Spelling Workout

Phillip K. Trocki

MODERN CURRICULUM PRESS

COVER DESIGN: Pronk & Associates

ILLUSTRATIONS: Rick Zwigleben

PHOTOGRAPHS: All photos © Pearson Learning unless otherwise noted.

Cover: Artbase Inc.

6: Darrell Gulin/Corbis. 9, 10: Stephen Frink/Corbis. 13: Bob Daemmrich/Stock Boston/PictureQuest. 14: Joseph Sohm/Chromosohm/Stock Connection/PictureQuest. 17: David Buffington/PhotoDisc, Inc. 18: Paul Kaye/Corbis. 21: David Young-Wolff/PictureQuest. 23: Laura Dwight/Corbis. 29: Joseph Sohm; Chromosohm Inc./Corbis. 30: AFP/Corbis. 33: Jonathan Nourok/PhotoEdit. 38: CMCD/PhotoDisc, Inc. 40: Will Hart Photography. 41: Roger Ressmeyer/Corbis. 45: The Purcell Team/Corbis. 46: Gale Zucker/Stock Boston. 51: Pictor International/Pictor International Ltd./PictureQuest. 53: Walter Choroszewski/PictureQuest. 54: Robert Holmes/Corbis. 57: Martin B. Withers/Frank Lane Picture Agency/Corbis. 58: Michael & Patricia Fogden/Corbis. 61: Robert Brenner/PhotoEdit. 62: AFP/Corbis. 65: T. Arruza/Bruce Coleman Incorporated. 67: Westlight Stock-OZ Productions/Corbis. 69: IFA Bilderteam/Stock Photography/PictureQuest. 75: C Squared Studios/PhotoDisc, Inc. 77: Bettmann/Corbis. 79: Culver Pictures/PictureQuest. 81: Peter Johnson/Corbis. 82: Galto Images/Corbis. 83: Picture Finders Ltd./PictureQuest. 86: Brian Cosgrove/Dorling Kindersley. 89: Will Hart Photography. 90: Morton Beebe, S.F./Corbis. 95: Kevin R. Morris/Corbis. 101: Gunter Marx/Corbis. 102: Ewing Galloway/Index Stock Imagery. 105: Ecoscene/Corbis. 106: Paul A. Saunders/Corbis. 108: Corbis. 109: Richard Hutchings/PhotoEdit. 113: Ted Spiegel/Corbis. 114: Pioneer Publications, Inc. 117: David A. Northcott/Corbis. 119: Lynda Richardson/Corbis. 125, 126: Jeffrey L. Rotman/Corbis. 133: Richard Nowitz Photography. 134: U.S. Space & Rocket Center/NASA. 138: Kim Taylor/Dorling Kindersley. 141: Bob Krist/Corbis. 142: Richard Bickel/Corbis.

Acknowledgments

ZB Font Method Copyright © 1996 Zaner-Bloser.

Some content in this product is based upon *Webster's New World Dictionary for Young Adults.* © 2001 Hungry Minds, Inc. All rights reserved. Webster's New World is a trademark or registered trademark of Hungry Minds, Inc.

NOTE: Every effort has been made to locate the copyright owner of material reprinted in this book. Omissions brought to our attention will be corrected in subsequent editions.

Copyright © 2002 by Pearson Education, Inc., publishing as Modern Curriculum Press, an imprint of Pearson Learning Group, 299 Jefferson Road, Parsippany, NJ 07054. All rights reserved. No part of this book may be reproduced or transmitted in any form or by any means, electronic or mechanical, including photocopying, recording, or by any information storage and retrieval system, without permission in writing from the publisher. For information regarding permission(s), write to Rights and Permissions Department.

ISBN 0-7652-2481-X

Printed in the United States of America.

9 10 07

1-800-321-3106
www.pearsonlearning.com

Table of Contents

Learning to Spell a Word

1. Say the word.
Look at the word and say the letters.

2. Write the word with your finger.

3. Close your eyes and think of the word.

4. Cover the word and write it.

5. Check your spelling.

Making a Spelling Notebook

Write your spelling words
in a **spelling notebook**.

Spelling Words in Action

How many letters are in the alphabet?

Alphabet Acrobat

There are 26 letters in the alphabet. Not long ago someone **saw** a way to use all 26 letters in one sentence. Here it is:

"The quick brown **fox** jumps over a lazy dog."

The sentence uses **all** 26 letters of the alphabet. See if you can find them all.

No one has been able to write a sentence using each letter just once. Can you **put** all the letters of the alphabet into one sentence? If your sentence has fewer than 33 letters, **tell** everyone you know. You may have set a **new** world record!

Look back at the words in dark print. Say each word. What consonant sounds do you hear?

Spelling Practice

TIP

Consonants are all the letters of the alphabet except **a, e, i, o, u,** and sometimes **y**. Each consonant spells its own sound. Listen for each sound in the **list words**.

LIST WORDS

1. fox
2. cut
3. hill
4. wind
5. put
6. all
7. moon
8. saw
9. tell
10. new

Writing Consonants

Write the missing consonants for each word. Trace the letters to spell **list words**.

1. ind
2. pu
3. aw
4. ox
5. ew
6. al
7. el
8. il
9. oo
10. cu

Missing Words

Write a **list word** to finish each sentence.

1. Last night, I saw a full ________ in the sky.
2. I thought the red, furry animal was a dog,

   but it was a ________.
3. She ________ the pencil in the drawer.
4. I pushed my go-cart to the top of the ________.

Word Puzzle

Read each clue. Write **list words** to fill in the puzzle.

Across

1. to use scissors
5. every one
6. not old

Down

2. to say
3. air that moves
4. used the eyes

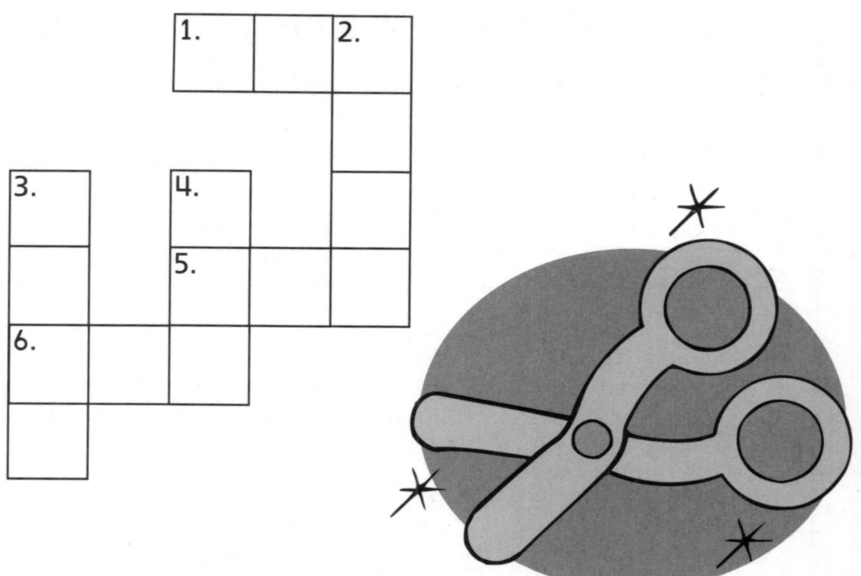

Spelling and Writing

Proofreading

Proofreading Marks

spelling mistake (circle)
⊙ add period

Each sentence has two mistakes. Use the proofreading marks to fix each mistake. Write the misspelled **list words** correctly on the lines.

1. Carl made a nue alphabet 1. ____________

2. He wrote down al the letters 2. ____________

3. Then he putt a picture next to each letter 3. ____________

Writing a Sentence

It's not easy to use every letter of the alphabet in one sentence. Try this instead. Write one sentence using as many **list words** as you can. Proofread your sentence. Fix any mistakes.

____

____

____

BONUS WORDS

bad
ball
fix
ear
trip

Spelling Words in Action

What are "marching molars"?

Did You Ever See a Manatee?

Manatees are big animals that live in water. They are gentle giants and love to play.

Manatees eat sea grasses and weeds. They **also** eat tree branches hanging close to the water.

Scientists studied manatees and discovered something special. When a manatee's front teeth wore out, they **fell** out! Then the teeth in the back moved toward the front. New teeth grew in the back. Scientists **had** never seen this before. They called these teeth "marching molars" because they are always "marching" from the back of the manatee's mouth to the front.

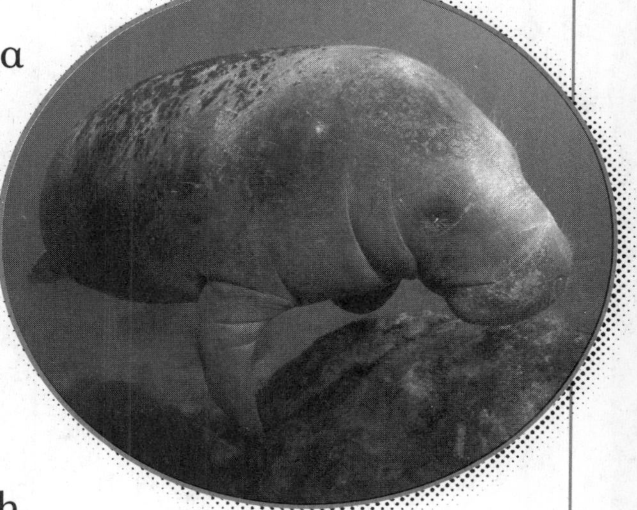

A manatee can live to be about 60 years **old**. **His** teeth are not nearly that old, though!

Look back at the words in dark print. Say each word. What consonant sounds do you hear?

Spelling Practice

Consonants are the building blocks of all words. Any letter that is not a vowel is a **consonant**. Listen for the sounds of the consonants in these words.

get **had** **took**

LIST WORDS

1. let
2. his
3. had
4. ask
5. old
6. took
7. also
8. sat
9. fell
10. get

Writing Consonants

Write the missing consonants for each word. Trace the letters to spell **list words**.

1. _ oo _
2. _ e _
3. _ e _
4. _ i _
5. _ a _
6. a _ _
7. a _ _ o
8. _ e _
9. o _ _
10. _ a _

Word Clues

Read each clue. Then write the **list word** that rhymes with the underlined word.

1. It means **allowed**.
   It rhymes with <u>pet</u>. ____________
2. It means **got hold of**.
   It rhymes with <u>look</u>. ____________
3. It means **used a chair**.
   It rhymes with <u>cat</u>. ____________
4. It means **go and bring something**.
   It rhymes with <u>net</u>. ____________

Story

Write **list words** to finish the story.

The Lion House

I saw a big lion at the zoo. When he opened ____________ mouth, I saw no teeth! I decided to ____________ about the lion. I was sure he ____________ teeth once. The zookeeper told me, "His teeth ____________ out. He is a very ____________ lion. We ____________ have some baby lions." I looked at the baby lions. They did not have teeth either!

Spelling and Writing

Proofreading

Each sentence has two mistakes. Use the proofreading marks to fix each mistake. Write the misspelled **list words** correctly on the lines.

Proofreading Marks

- ⬭ spelling mistake
- ≡ capital letter

1. sally, the olt giraffe, was crying. 1. ____________

2. Doctor allen tuk a look at Sally's eyes. 2. ____________

3. the giraffe hed an eyelash in its eye. 3. ____________

Writing a Story

Write a story about a visit to the dentist. Tell what the dentist did to your teeth. Use as many **list words** as you can. Proofread your story. Fix any mistakes.

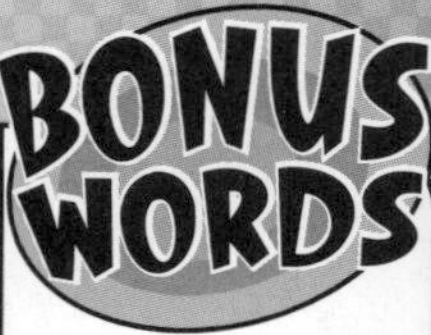

- look
- cold
- blue
- ship
- mask

Spelling Words in Action

Why is it important to have the right equipment?

Be Prepared

It is important to **have** the right sports equipment. Is your baseball **mitt** the right size? You **will** find it hard to catch those fly balls if your mitt is too big.

If your sneakers do not **fit** right, you might fall and **skin** your knee. That would make you **sad**.

On hot days, you might use a sweat **band**. This cloth band fits around the top of your head. It keeps sweat from running down your face or into your eyes.

When a sports season starts, make a **list** of what you will need. Make sure you always have the right equipment.

Say each word in dark print in the paragraphs. What vowel sounds do you hear?

Spelling Practice

TIP

Each **list word** has the short **a** sound or the short **i** sound. You hear the short **i** sound in fit. You hear the short **a** sound in sad and in have, even though have has more than one vowel.

LIST WORDS

1. band
2. fit
3. him
4. tack
5. sad
6. list
7. mitt
8. have
9. will
10. skin

Identifying Short Vowel Sounds

Write each **list word** under the heading that shows its short vowel sound.

a as in cat

1. ____________ 2. ____________

3. ____________ 4. ____________

i as in sit

5. ____________ 6. ____________

7. ____________ 8. ____________

9. ____________ 10. ____________

Opposites

Write a **list word** that means the opposite of each word.

1. won't ____________
2. happy ____________
3. her ____________
4. haven't ____________

Rhyming

Write a **list word** to match each clue.

1. These two **list words** rhyme with each other. ____________ ____________
2. This word rhymes with thin. ____________
3. This word rhymes with back. ____________
4. This word rhymes with fist. ____________
5. This word rhymes with hand. ____________

Spelling and Writing

Proofreading

Proofreading Marks

- ⬭ spelling mistake
- ⊙ add period

Each sentence has two mistakes. Use the proofreading marks to fix each mistake. Write the misspelled **list words** correctly on the lines.

1. I hav gloves to keep my hands warm — 1. ________

2. My mit helps me catch baseballs — 2. ________

3. My mittens fitt over my fingers like a sock — 3. ________

Writing a Description

Describe something you wear on your hands. Try to use as many **list words** as you can. Proofread your description. Fix any mistakes.

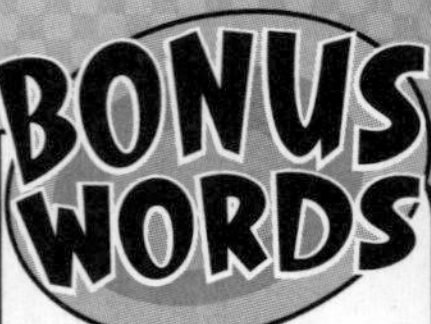

bit
gift
pad
stand
rack

Spelling Words in Action

Can you think of a word that is spelled the same backward and forward?

Inside Out

In English, words are spelled from left to right. You **must** always spell them that way.

Some words are spelled the same backward or forward. Spell **pup** backward. It still spells p-u-p. Pop is still pop. Mom is always mom. Can you think of some others?

Try some spelling magic. With backward spelling, some words become other words. The word **tug** becomes gut. A **pot** becomes a top. With backward magic, a bus can go underwater because it turns into a sub.

When you spell **frog** backward, you get gorf. Gorf is not a real word. It sounds funny, though. Try to make up a funny meaning for your new nonsense word.

Look back at the words in dark print. Say each word. How many different vowel sounds do you hear?

Each **list word** has the short **u** sound or the short **o** sound. You hear the short **u** sound in must and pup. You hear the short **o** sound in soft and pot.

Spelling Practice

LIST WORDS

1. gum
2. pot
3. dust
4. frog
5. must
6. sock
7. pup
8. shot
9. soft
10. tug

Identifying Short Vowel Sounds

Write each **list word** under the heading that shows its short-vowel sound.

u as in up

1. ______ 2. ______
3. ______ 4. ______
5. ______

o as in hot

6. ______ 7. ______
8. ______ 9. ______
10. ______

Missing Words

Look at the pictures. Write a **list word** to finish each sentence.

1. The ______________ cleans his house.

2. He cooks in a ______________.

3. He eats with his pal the ______________.

Word Puzzle

Read each clue. Write **list words** to fill in the puzzle.

Across

1. What you like a pillow to be.
3. People chew this.
6. I ___ an arrow into the target.

Down

1. You wear this on your foot.
2. This means to pull.
4. I ___ eat a good breakfast each day.
5. This can make you sneeze.

Spelling and Writing

Proofreading

Proofreading Marks

- (oval) spelling mistake
- (triple underline) capital letter

Each sentence has two mistakes. Use the proofreading marks to fix each mistake. Write the misspelled **list words** correctly on the lines.

1. Carla has a pupp named snowball. 1. ____________
2. snowball's favorite toy is an old sok. 2. ____________
3. carla and her pup play tuge of war with it. 3. ____________

Writing a Story

Some people can swim backwards. Sometimes cars and trucks drive backwards. Write a story about something you think would be fun to do backwards. Proofread your story. Fix any mistakes.

BONUS WORDS

- stuck
- stop
- fog
- just
- lock

Spelling Words in Action

What are white and can bite?

Shiny White, Shiny Bright

There's a **set** of things inside your **head**.
They're strong. They're hard. They bite!
They're shiny, small, and when you smile,
they make a lovely sight.

At school and home, they **help** you speak.
They help you chew your **bread**.
They chatter when the day is cold.
They're white, not blue or red.

Brush them before you go to **bed**,
and floss them, don't forget!
Brushing after every meal is even
better **yet**.

Just remember what I **said**,
and you'll keep your teeth inside your head.

Look back at the words in dark print. Say each word. What vowel sound do you hear in each word?

Spelling Practice

Each **list word** spells the short **e** sound in one of these ways:
e, as in set and help
ea, as in head
ai, as in said

LIST WORDS

1. set
2. head
3. help
4. yet
5. bread
6. belt
7. tent
8. said
9. bed
10. sell

Writing the Short e Sound

Write the missing letter or letters that make the **e** sound in the words. Trace the letters to spell **list words**.

1. 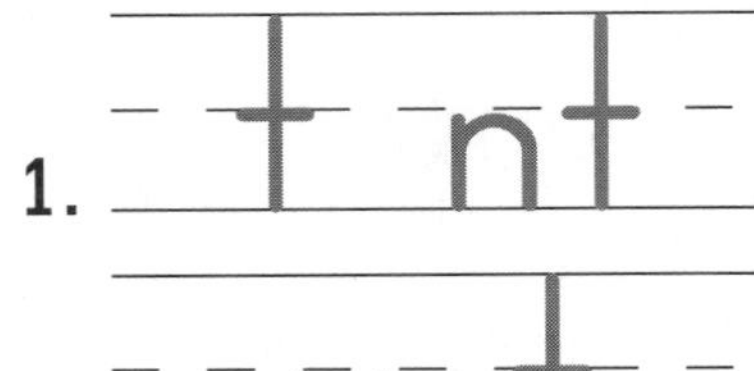

2. 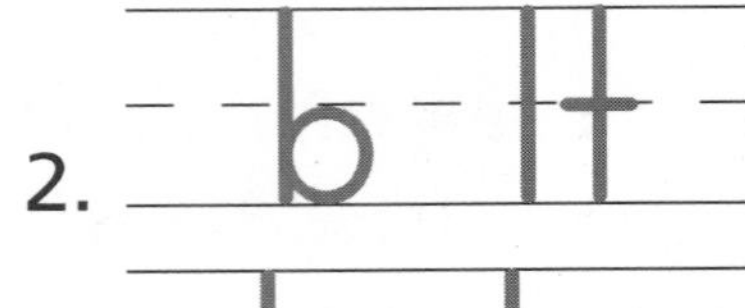

3. 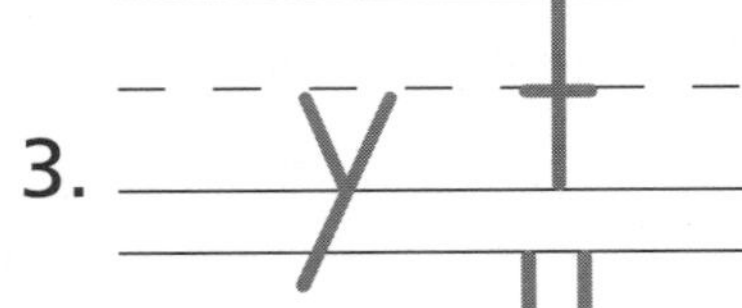

4. 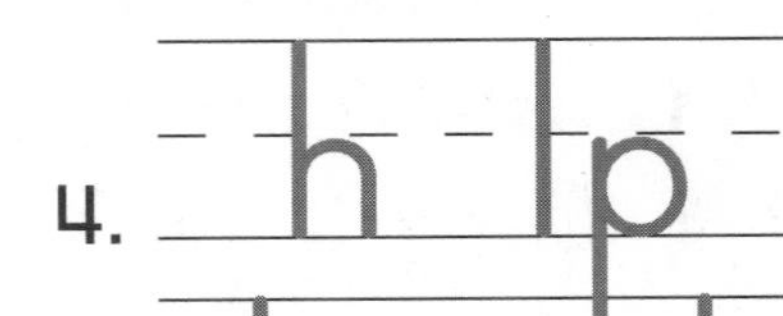

5. 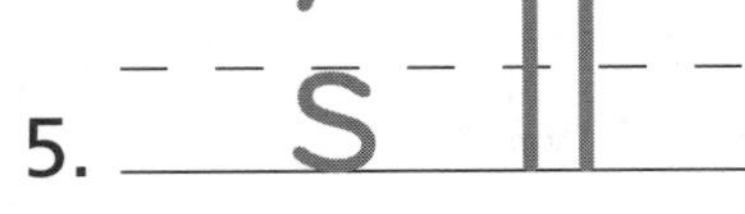

6. 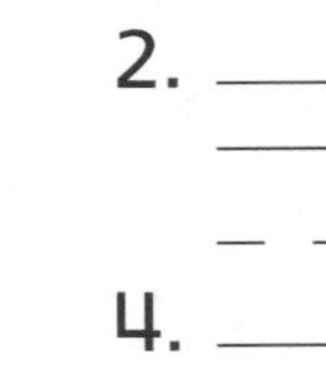 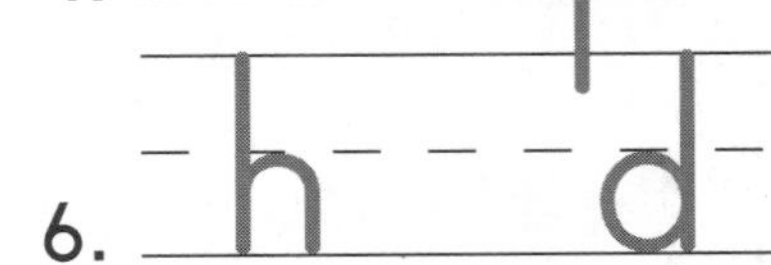

7. 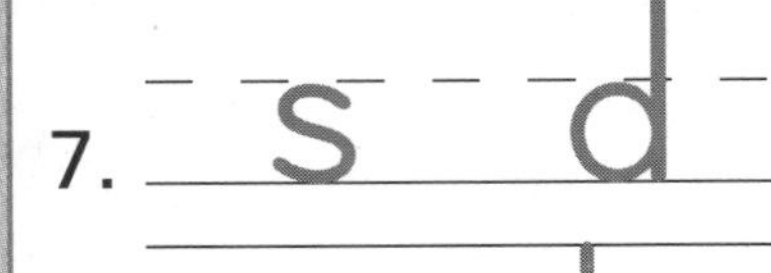

8. 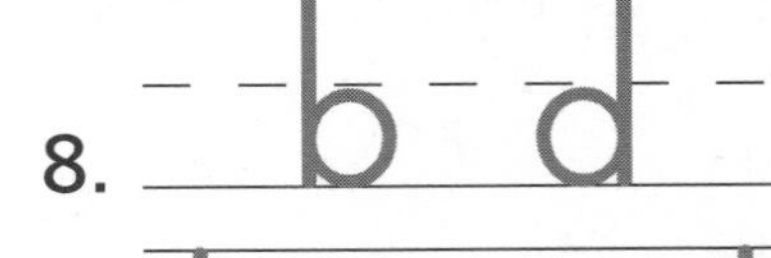

9. 

10. br d

Riddle Puzzle

Read each clue. Write **list words** to fill in the puzzle.

1. This means to give something for money.
2. You need this when you're in trouble.
3. This word means up to now.
4. This is worn around the waist.
5. This is a good place to sleep.
6. This is a food made with flour.
7. You may use this to camp out.
8. This holds your brain.

Now read down the shaded boxes to find the answer to the riddle. Write it on the lines.

Riddle: You have to lose one to get number two. If you didn't have any, you just couldn't chew. What is it?

Answer: a ________ of ________

Story

Write **list words** to finish the story.

I went to ________ at seven-thirty. I ________ the clock. I ________, "Good night."

Spelling and Writing

Proofreading

Proofreading Marks

⬭ spelling mistake
⊙ add period

Each sentence has two mistakes. Use the proofreading marks to fix each mistake. Write the misspelled **list words** correctly on the lines.

1. Doctors have not yat found a cure for the common cold

2. They have sade you should keep your body warm

3. Also, try to stay in bedde for at least one whole day

1. ______________

2. ______________

3. ______________

Making a Poster

It's important to take care of your teeth. Make a poster that shows how. Write your first draft on the lines. Use as many **list words** as you can. Proofread your poster. Fix any mistakes.

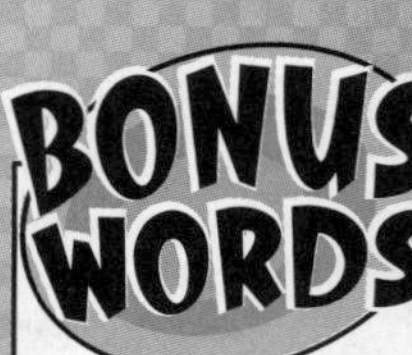

pet
heavy
spread
met
led

Lessons 1–5 • Review

In Lessons 1 through 5, you learned to spell words with consonants and short vowel sounds.

Check Your Spelling Notebook

Look at the words in your spelling notebook. Which words for Lessons 1 through 5 did you have the most trouble with? Write them here.

Lesson 1

Any letter that is not a vowel is a consonant. Listen for the consonant sounds in these words: fox, wind.

Write a **list word** that rhymes with each word.

List Words

- moon
- all
- new
- saw

1. soon
2. jaw
3. chew
4. ball

Lesson 2

Consonants are the building blocks for all words. Listen for the consonant sounds in these words: took, also.

List Words

ask
old
his
get

Write a **list word** that means the opposite of each word.

1. hers ____________ 2. give ____________

3. new ____________ 4. answer ____________

Lesson 3

You can hear the short a sound in band and sad. Listen for the short i sound in fit and skin.

List Words

have
tack
mitt
will

Write a **list word** to finish each sentence.

1. We ____________ go now.

2. Let's ____________ a party.

3. You can ____________ up the sign.

4. This is my baseball ____________.

Lesson 4

TIP **Some words have the short u sound or the short o sound. Listen for the short u sound in gum and must. Listen for the short o sound in pot and sock.**

List Words

frog
soft
pup
tug

Write a **list word** that means the same or almost the same as each word.

1. pull ____________
2. toad ____________
3. dog ____________
4. gentle ____________

Lesson 5

TIP **The short e sound is spelled in different ways: e, as in help; ea, as in bread; and ai, as in said.**

List Words

head
set
said
tent

Write a **list word** to match each clue.

1. You do this to the dinner table. ____________
2. You sleep here on a camping trip. ____________
3. This word means the same as spoke. ____________
4. This is at the top of your body. ____________

Show What You Know

Lessons 1–5 Review

One word is misspelled in each set of **list words**. Fill in the circle next to the **list word** that is spelled incorrectly.

1.	○ fit	○ foks	○ hill	○ tack
2.	○ gom	○ pup	○ put	○ new
3.	○ bed	○ sett	○ saw	○ will
4.	○ head	○ let	○ sad	○ healp
5.	○ list	○ winde	○ tent	○ all
6.	○ sock	○ old	○ skin	○ kut
7.	○ get	○ tell	○ new	○ brede
8.	○ touk	○ dust	○ ask	○ also
9.	○ fox	○ sell	○ lisst	○ moon
10.	○ set	○ mitt	○ hiz	○ him
11.	○ will	○ fel	○ band	○ frog
12.	○ hav	○ had	○ sat	○ yet
13.	○ must	○ bed	○ shot	○ bellt
14.	○ took	○ pot	○ saft	○ all
15.	○ cut	○ auld	○ tug	○ sad
16.	○ hil	○ help	○ mitt	○ wind
17.	○ sell	○ fell	○ frogg	○ his
18.	○ have	○ sat	○ schot	○ sock
19.	○ said	○ soft	○ gum	○ muon
20.	○ tugg	○ belt	○ bread	○ put

Spelling Words in Action

What kind of car would you like to drive someday?

Future Cars

Driving will never be the **same** again! Amazing new cars are changing the **face** of driving. The Skycar won't get stuck in traffic jams. It will **sail** right over them. The Skycar can lift off straight into the air. It can land the same way.

Some people are **afraid** to fly. They might like a car that swims. It goes from highway to **lake** with no problem. That could **save** drivers a lot of time.

Some drivers could save money, too. The Solar Phantom has special panels. The panels allow the car to run on sunlight instead of gas.

These are some of the cars of the future. Who knows? Maybe you will design an amazing car yourself someday.

Look back at the words in dark print. Say each word. What vowel sound do you hear?

Spelling Practice

TIP

The long **a** sound is the vowel sound you hear in save and sail. Each **list word** has the long **a** sound spelled in one of these ways: **a_e** or **ai**.

LIST WORDS

1. save
2. lake
3. face
4. same
5. gate
6. rake
7. tape
8. sail
9. paint
10. afraid

Writing the Long a Sound

Write each **list word** under the heading that shows its long **a** spelling pattern.

ai

1. ______________ 2. ______________

3. ______________

a_e

4. ______________ 5. ______________

6. ______________ 7. ______________

8. ______________ 9. ______________

10. ______________

Mixed Up Words

The underlined **list word** in each sentence does not make sense. Write the **list word** that does make sense on the line.

1. It is fun to swim in the <u>paint</u>. ____________

2. I help my mother <u>tape</u> leaves in the fall. ____________

3. Open the <u>sail</u> to enter the garden. ____________

4. I <u>face</u> the planet by recycling. ____________

Word Puzzle

Read each clue.
Write **list words** to fill in the puzzle.

Across

3. scared
5. It has eyes, a nose, and a mouth.
6. This makes things stick together.
8. This catches the wind on a boat.
9. a door in a fence

Down

1. take leaves off the grass
2. a kind of big pond
4. alike
7. This is one way to color a picture.
8. put money in a bank

Spelling and Writing

Proofreading

Proofreading Marks

- (oval) spelling mistake
- (three lines) capital letter
- (circled dot) add period

Each sentence has two mistakes. Use the proofreading marks to fix each mistake. Write the misspelled **list words** correctly on the lines.

1. The boat with the red sale was sam's. 1. ____________

2. it flew across the lak. 2. ____________

3. Sam wasn't afrade, and he won the race 3. ____________

Writing a News Story

A good news story always tells who or what the story is about and where and when it happened. Write a news story about someone who did a good deed. Then proofread your news story and fix any mistakes.

____

____

____

____

BONUS WORDS

plane
bait
brave
tame
trail

Spelling Words in Action

What is your favorite kind of race?

Friends Come First

Mike stood on **line** for the bike race. The race was one **mile** long, and the prizes were great. It would be **nice** to win one.

Mike felt a tap on his arm. His best friend, Sarah, was **behind** him. She wore a **wide** smile on her face. "I knew I would **find** you here," she said. "I am racing, too."

It was a **fine** day for a race. Would Mike's red bike be as fast as a **fire** engine? The race began. Mike pedaled as hard as he could.

"You can't **hide** from me!" Sarah called. Soon, her bike was next to Mike's. Mike pedaled even faster.

At last, Mike zoomed past the finish line a few inches ahead of Sarah. Mike won the race!

"Congratulations!" Sarah told him. "I don't **mind** losing so much because my best friend won."

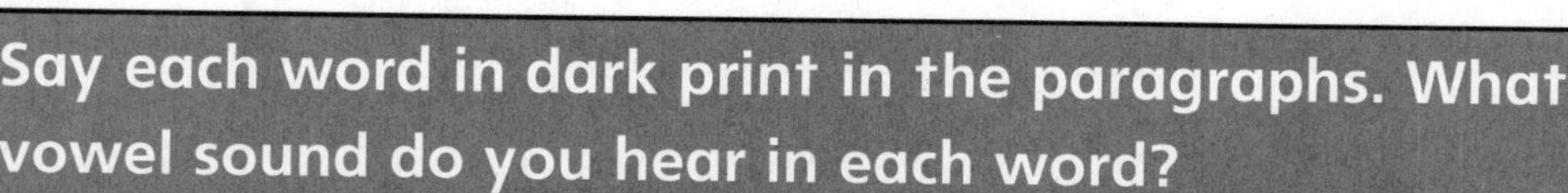

Spelling Practice

Each **list word** has the long **i** sound. Sometimes the sound is spelled **i_e**, as in mile. Sometimes the long **i** is spelled **i _ _**, as in find.

LIST WORDS

1. wide
2. mile
3. line
4. hide
5. fire
6. nice
7. fine
8. mind
9. find
10. behind

Spelling the Long i Sound

Write each **list word** under the heading that shows its long **i** spelling pattern.

i_e

1. ____________ 2. ____________
3. ____________ 4. ____________
5. ____________ 6. ____________
7. ____________

i _ _

8. ____________ 9. ____________
10. ____________

Word Clues

Write the **list word** that matches each clue.

1. This means kind. ____________
2. You use this to think. ____________
3. It is hot. Be careful! ____________
4. Can you run this far? ____________
5. This tells how you feel. ____________
6. This means in back of. ____________

Missing Words

Write a **list word** to finish each sentence.

1. The ____________ for the movie is very long.
2. I hope we can ____________ good seats.
3. This is a very ____________ movie screen.
4. If the movie is scary, I will ____________ under my chair.

Spelling and Writing

Proofreading

Proofreading Marks

- ⬭ spelling mistake
- ⊙ add period

Each sentence has two mistakes. Use the proofreading marks to fix each mistake. Write the misspelled **list words** correctly on the lines.

1. I keep these rules in min when I ride a bike

2. I stay on whyd roads

3. I use a mirror to see behine me

1. ________

2. ________

3. ________

Writing a Paragraph

Remember the day you learned how to do something for the first time? Write a paragraph telling about that day. Proofread your paragraph. Fix any mistakes.

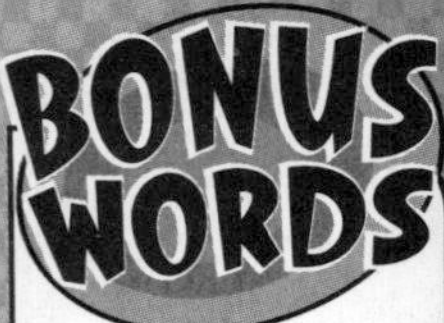

wire
pipe
pint
bite
kind

Spelling Words in Action

What are nachos?

A Fun Snack

It's **true**! Nachos are fun to make and fun to eat. Here's a recipe to make nachos for **you** and a **few** of your amigos. (Amigos is Spanish for friends.)

First, you will need a grown-up to help you. You will also need a package of corn chips, a large baking dish, and some grated cheese. **Use** Monterey Jack cheese or cheddar.

Heat the oven to 350 degrees. Spread the corn chips around in the bottom of the baking dish. Sprinkle the cheese over the chips. Bake in the oven for about 10 minutes until the cheese is melted. Be sure to use an oven mitt when you take your nachos out of the oven. That's an important **rule**! Let the nachos cool for a bit and dig in. Mmmmm.

Say each word in dark print in the paragraphs. What vowel sound do you hear?

Spelling Practice

TIP

Each list word has a long **u** sound. The long **u** can be spelled **ew**, as in few; **u_e**, as in rule; **ue**, as in true; and **ou**, as in you.

LIST WORDS

1. rule
2. use
3. tune
4. mule
5. due
6. true
7. grew
8. few
9. you
10. cute

Writing the Long u Sounds

Write each **list word** under the heading that shows its long **u** sound spelling.

u_e, as in June

1. ______________ 2. ______________

3. ______________ 4. ______________

5. ______________

ew, as in new

6. ______________ 7. ______________

ue, as in blue

8. ______________ 9. ______________

ou, as in soup

10. ______________

Mixed Up Words

The underlined **list word** in each sentence does not make sense. Write the **list word** that does make sense.

1. We sang a happy rule in our holiday concert. ______________
2. My spelling homework is true tomorrow. ______________
3. I want to tune the phone. ______________
4. "Be kind to others," is a good mule. ______________
5. The story was cute and also grew. ______________

Story

Write **list words** to complete the story.

My pet ______________ is smaller than a horse. When he was a baby, his fuzzy ears were so ______________. When he ______________ bigger, his ears looked different. I've only ridden my mule a ______________ times. ______________ can ride him, too.

Spelling and Writing

Proofreading

Proofreading Marks

⬭	spelling mistake
≡	capital letter
^	add something

Each sentence has two mistakes. Use the proofreading marks to fix them. Write the misspelled **list words** correctly on the lines.

1. Do you want the myool to sing to you
2. she will sing her favorite toon.
3. her voice changed as she grue up.

1. ______
2. ______
3. ______

Writing a Recipe

A finger food is a snack you eat with your fingers, such as nachos. What other finger food do you like? Tell what it is and how to make it.

BONUS WORDS

knew
threw
clue
tube
huge

Spelling Words in Action

Who invented the yo-yo?

One of the Oldest Toys in the World

No one knows who invented the yo-yo. Children in ancient Greece played with yo-yos 2,500 years **ago**. In the 1800s, grown-ups in France had yo-yos of their **own**. Today, yo-yos are **sold** all **over** the world.

If you **go** to a museum, you may see some old pictures of yo-yos. **Those** old yo-yos were made of wood or clay. Some were made of metal.

In the Philippines, the word yo-yo means to bounce back. Yo-yos were popular there for hundreds of years. Then Pedro Flores moved to California from the Philippines. He opened a yo-yo factory in 1928. It started a yo-yo craze in this country. If you have a yo-yo, you have Pedro Flores to thank.

Look back at the words in dark print. Say each word. Do you hear the long o sound in each word?

Spelling Practice

Each **list word** has the long **o** sound, spelled in one of the following five ways: **o_e**, as in those; **ow**, as in low; **oa**, as in coat; **o**, as in go; or **old**, as in sold.

LIST WORDS

1. those
2. low
3. goat
4. own
5. coat
6. go
7. hope
8. sold
9. over
10. ago

Writing the Long o Sound

Write the missing letter or letters for the long **o** sound in each word. Trace the letters to spell **list words**.

1. ___n
2. ___ver
3. ag___
4. l___
5. g___
6. s___
7. th___s___
8. h___p___
9. c___t
10. g___t

Opposites

Write the **list word** that means the opposite of each word.

1. under ______
2. stop ______
3. high ______
4. bought ______
5. these ______
6. now long

Alphabetical Order

Circle the **list words** in the silly rhyme.
Then write the words in ABC order.

I hope you see
the funny old goat
in its very own coat
who went to sea
in a motorboat.

1. ______
2. ______
3. ______

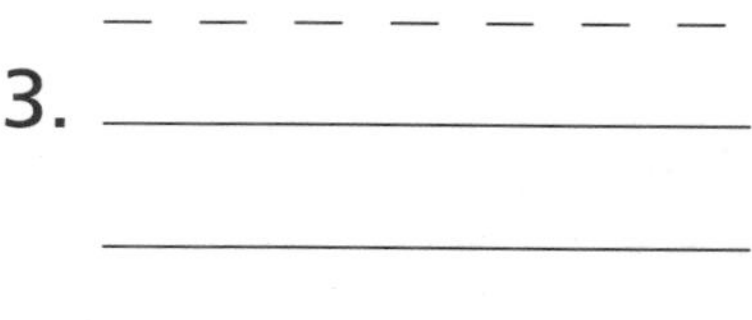

4. ______

Spelling and Writing

Proofreading

Each sentence has two mistakes. Use the proofreading marks to fix each mistake. Write the misspelled **list words** correctly on the lines.

Proofreading Marks

- spelling mistake (oval)
- ^ add something

1. How many millions of teddy bears do you think have been solde
2. Do you know that even grown-ups owne teddy bears
3. Why do you think thoes bears are so popular

1. ______
2. ______
3. ______

Writing a Description

Write about your favorite toy. Tell when you got it, how it works, and what it does. Use as many **list words** as you can. Proofread your description. Fix any mistakes.

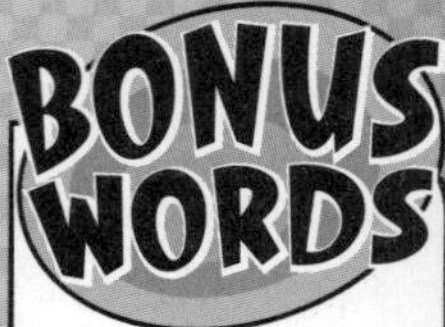

fold
so
nose
boat
blow

Spelling Words in Action

What is green, breathes air, and lives in water?

Making It on Their Own

Green **sea** turtles are reptiles. They live in the ocean, but they are born on land.

A mother sea turtle crawls onto a **beach** when she is ready to lay her eggs. She lays her eggs and goes back into the water.

When the baby turtles hatch, they are on their own. First they must crawl into the sea. It is not **easy** for them to get there. Sea turtles move very slowly on land. This puts them in **real** danger. They may **meet** a hungry seagull or crab along the way. These animals will **feed** on baby sea turtles. Still, the baby turtles **keep** on crawling.

When the baby turtles reach the sea, they swim for one or two days to get to **deep** water. In deep water, the baby turtles are safe.

Say each word in dark print in the paragraphs. What vowel sound do you hear?

Spelling Practice

The long **e** sound is the vowel sound you hear in feed and sea. Each **list word** has the long **e** sound spelled in one of these ways: **ee** or **ea**.

LIST WORDS

1. feed
2. sea
3. meet
4. real
5. keep
6. week
7. deep
8. easy
9. beach
10. clean

Writing the Long e Sound

Write the missing letters for the long **e** sound in each word. Trace the letters to spell **list words**.

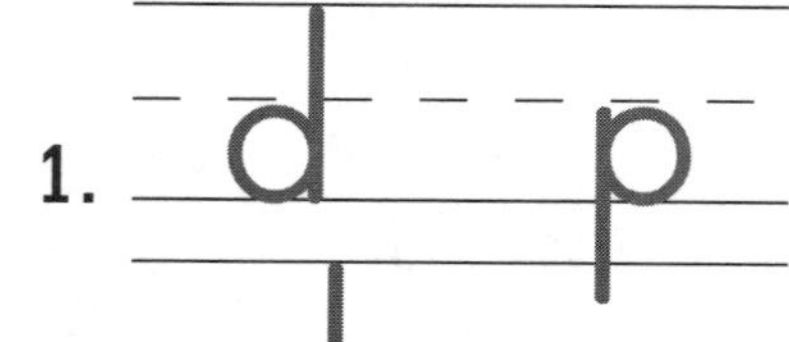

1. d __ __ p
2. __ __ sy
3. cl __ __ n
4. s __ __

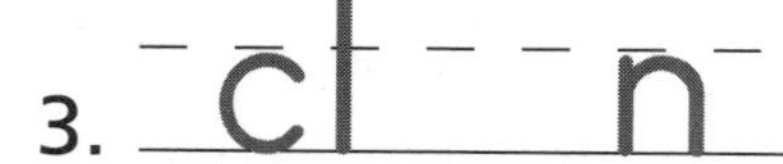

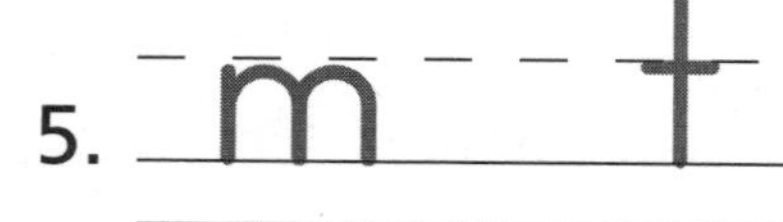

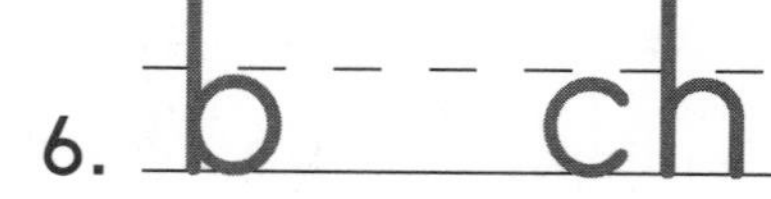

5. m __ __ t
6. b __ __ ch

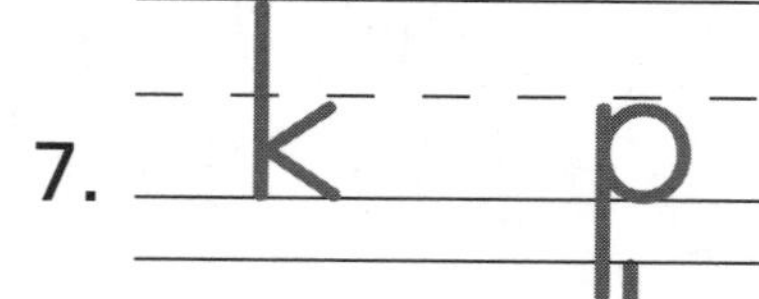

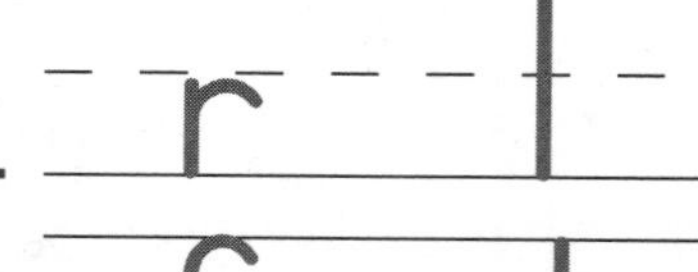

7. k __ __ p
8. r __ __ l
9. w __ __ k
10. f __ __ d

Opposites

Write the **list word** that means the opposite of each word.

1. dirty ______________
2. lose ______________
3. fake ______________
4. shallow ______________
5. hard ______________
6. starve ______________

Rhyming Clues

Read each clue. Then write the **list word** that rhymes.

1. It is seven days.
   It rhymes with peek. ______________
2. This is sand by the ocean.
   It rhymes with teach. ______________
3. This is salty water.
   It rhymes with tea. ______________
4. This is when you see someone.
   It rhymes with feet. ______________

Spelling and Writing

Proofreading

Proofreading Marks

⬭ spelling mistake

⊙ add period

Each sentence has two mistakes. Use the proofreading marks to fix each mistake. Write the misspelled **list words** correctly on the lines.

1. Snapping turtles don't live in the see

2. You might mete one in a river or lake

3. If you see one, kepe away from its strong jaws

1. ____________

2. ____________

3. ____________

Writing a Journal Entry

Write a journal entry telling what you would like to do at a beach or lake. Proofread your work. Fix any mistakes.

sheep
sleep
heat
heel
teach

Lessons 7–11 • Review

In Lessons 7–11, you learned how to spell words with long vowel sounds.

Check Your Spelling Notebook

Look at the words in your spelling notebook. Which words for Lessons 7 through 11 did you have the most trouble with? Write them here.

Lesson 7

TIP **The long a sound can be spelled a_e, as in lake, and ai, as in afraid.**

Write the **list word** that belongs in each group.

List Words

face
save
paint
sail

1. brush, picture, ______

2. eyes, nose, ______

3. money, bank, ______

4. boat, water, ______

Lesson 8

TIP **Sometimes the long i sound is spelled i_e, as in hide. Other times it is spelled i_ _, as in find.**

List Words

- mind
- line
- nice
- mile

Write a **list word** that rhymes with each word.

1. smile ______
2. twice ______
3. kind ______
4. mine ______

Lesson 9

TIP **The long u sound can be spelled ue, as in due; u_e, as in use; and ew, as in grew.**

List Words

- few
- true
- cute
- tune

Write a **list word** to match each clue.

1. pretty ______
2. not many ______
3. song ______
4. not false ______

Lesson 10

TIP The long o sound can be spelled in five different ways: hope, own, goat, go, and sold.

List Words

coat
over
low
sold

Write a **list word** to finish each sentence.

1. This is a ______________ bridge.

2. They ______________ lemonade.

3. Hang up your ______________ .

4. Jump ______________ the rope.

Lesson 11

TIP Sometimes the long e sound is spelled ee, as in feed. Other times it is spelled ea, as in sea.

List Words

clean
keep
easy
real

Write the **list words** in alphabetical order.

1. ______________

2. ______________

3. ______________

4. ______________

Show What You Know

Lessons 7–11 Review

One word is misspelled in each set of **list words.** Fill in the circle next to the **list word** that is spelled incorrectly.

1.	○ owne	○ sea	○ tune	○ go
2.	○ paint	○ wide	○ raik	○ deep
3.	○ mind	○ lak	○ rule	○ mile
4.	○ sail	○ over	○ yu	○ feed
5.	○ due	○ tape	○ cute	○ lin
6.	○ eazy	○ hide	○ true	○ face
7.	○ hope	○ grew	○ afrayd	○ few
8.	○ mule	○ meet	○ cleen	○ fire
9.	○ behin	○ ago	○ coat	○ low
10.	○ goat	○ reall	○ use	○ week
11.	○ keap	○ nice	○ gate	○ those
12.	○ fine	○ sold	○ sav	○ same
13.	○ beach	○ finde	○ due	○ wide
14.	○ sea	○ hide	○ mil	○ line
15.	○ own	○ ago	○ afraid	○ taip
16.	○ rake	○ keep	○ soled	○ use
17.	○ clean	○ fayce	○ coat	○ fire
18.	○ deap	○ over	○ easy	○ find
19.	○ you	○ paint	○ mule	○ trew
20.	○ loe	○ save	○ few	○ mind

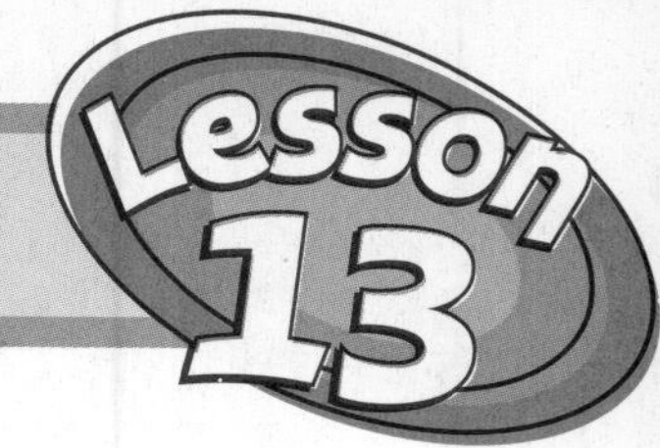

Spelling Words in Action

How tall is General Sherman?

Wooden Soldier

The day of the **class** trip was finally here. The students followed their teacher across the **grass**. A bird flew overhead. They all looked up. Then they saw it. The tree was huge. Its **trunk** was as wide as a **truck** is long.

The students were visiting Sequoia National Park in California. They were looking at the tallest tree in the world. It is a sequoia named General Sherman. It is 272 feet tall. The students looked up **from** the **flat** land around the tree. It was like looking at a 20-story building.

General Sherman is still growing in Sequoia National Park. Maybe you will visit it someday.

Look back at the words in dark print. What do you notice about their spelling? Say each word. What consonant sounds do you hear?

Spelling Practice

In a consonant **blend**, two or more consonants come together in a word. The sound of each consonant can be heard. You can hear the **l** blend in class and the **r** blend in grass.

LIST WORDS

1. grass
2. trunk
3. truck
4. flew
5. flat
6. class
7. plate
8. from
9. glove
10. friend

Identifying l and r Blends

Write each **list word** under the heading that shows its blend.

l blend

1. ____________ 2. ____________

3. ____________ 4. ____________

5. ____________

r blend

6. ____________ 7. ____________

8. ____________ 9. ____________

10. ____________

Word Groups

Write the **list word** that belongs with each group of words.

1. hat, coat, ______
2. pal, buddy, ______
3. spoon, glass, ______
4. school, teacher, ______
5. car, bus, ______
6. box, chest, ______

Scrambled Letters

Unscramble the letters to spell **list words**. The word shapes will help you.

1. morf
2. sargs 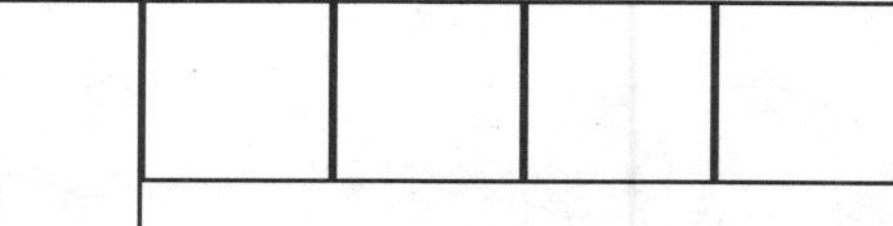
3. falt
4. welf 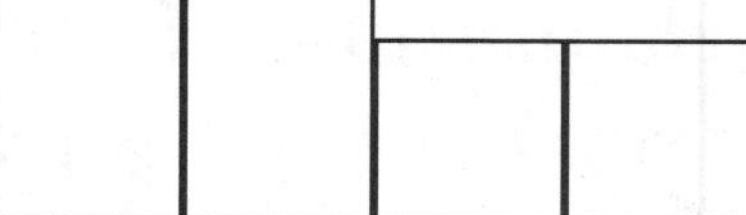
5. renifd 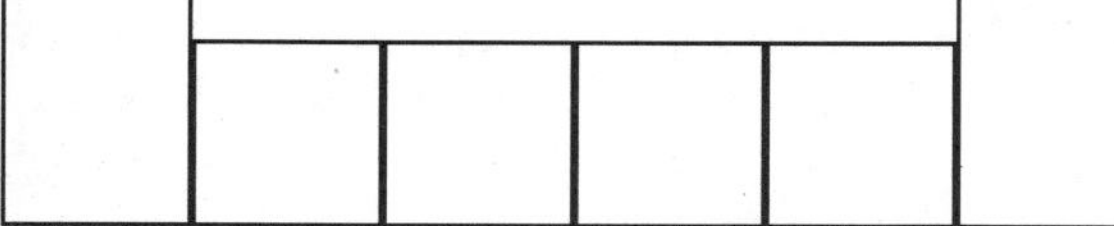
6. kurct

Spelling and Writing

Proofreading

Proofreading Marks

- (oval) spelling mistake
- (triple underline) capital letter

Each sentence has two mistakes. Use the proofreading marks to fix each mistake. Write the misspelled **list words** correctly on the lines.

1. Jackie bought a flate piece of land in oregon.
2. it has lots of green grase.
3. My frend jackie likes it there.

1. ____________
2. ____________
3. ____________

Writing a Poem

Trees give us shade, fruit, and branches to climb. Write a poem about a tree. Proofread your poem and fix any mistakes.

____

____

____

____

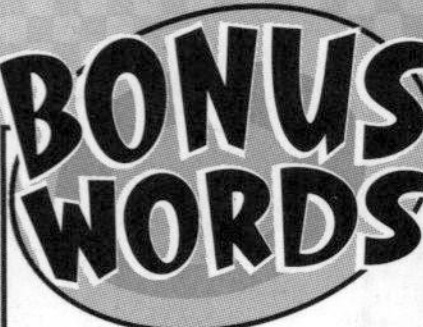

growl
fresh
plan
blanket
crown

Spelling Words in Action

What should you do if you see a snake?

Hissss!

Have you ever seen a **snake**? There are over 2,000 kinds of snakes. Water snakes **swim** in oceans, lakes, and rivers. Land snakes stay on the ground. Many people are afraid of snakes, but **most** snakes are harmless.

If you see a snake, stand very **still**. A snake will only **strike** at you if you come too close.

Snakes are different from other animals. They use their tongues to help them **smell**. Their tongues can also feel fast movements. Most snakes are helpful. They eat bugs and other pests. When you see a snake, just walk slowly away.

Say each word in dark print in the paragraphs. What consonant blend with s do you hear in each word?

Spelling Practice

TIP

The letter **s** can work with two or more letters to make a blend, as in still and strike. A blend can begin a word or end a word. Listen for the **s** blend in each **list word**.

LIST WORDS

1. snake
2. smell
3. still
4. smoke
5. spell
6. swim
7. slice
8. most
9. strike
10. story

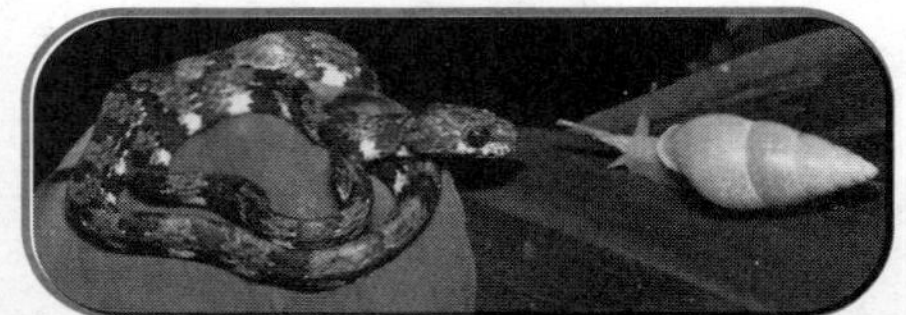

Identifying s Blends

Write each **list word** under the heading that shows its **s** blend.

st

1. ______________ 2. ______________

3. ______________

str

4. ______________

sp

5. ______________

sn

6. ______________

sl

7. ______________

sm

8. ______________ 9. ______________

sw

10. ______________

Missing Words

Write a **list word** to finish each sentence.

1. The person who gets the ____________ points wins.

2. ____________ the ball with the bat.

3. I ____________ chocolate chip cookies.

Scrambled Letters

Unscramble the letters to spell **list words**. The word shapes will help you. Then use the number code to answer the riddle.

1. msiw 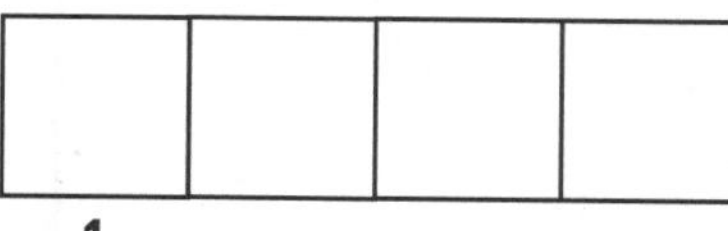

2. plels 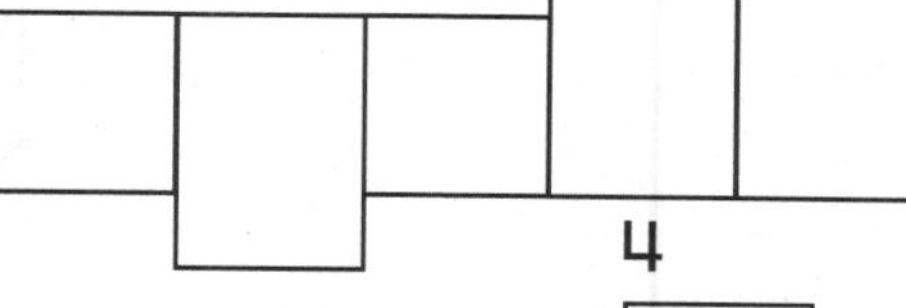

3. cseil 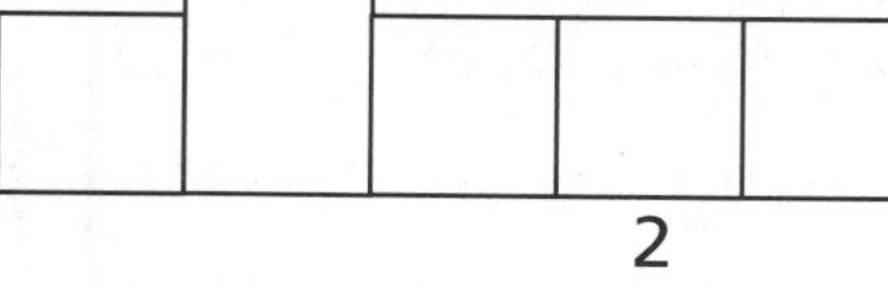

4. oekms 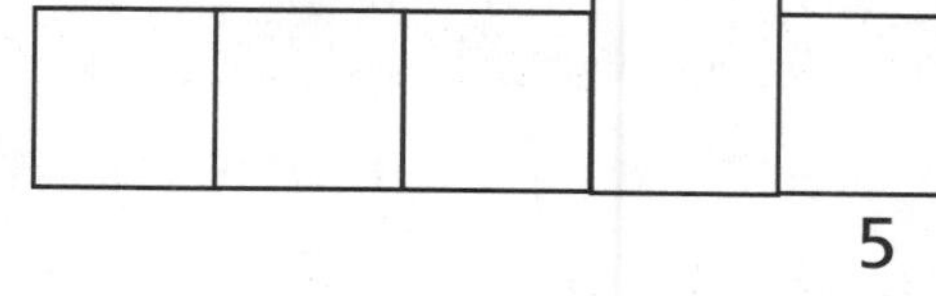

5. eksan 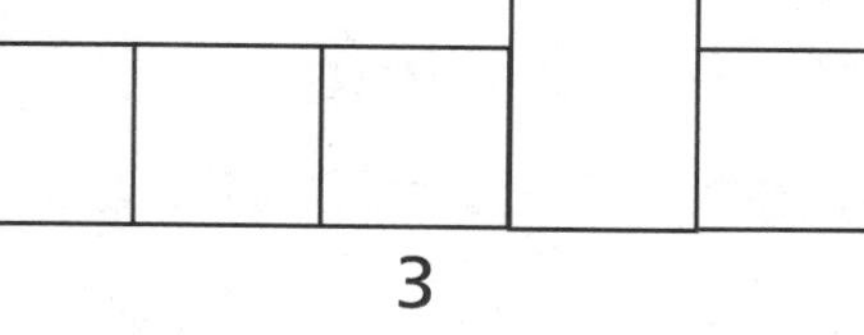

6. syrto 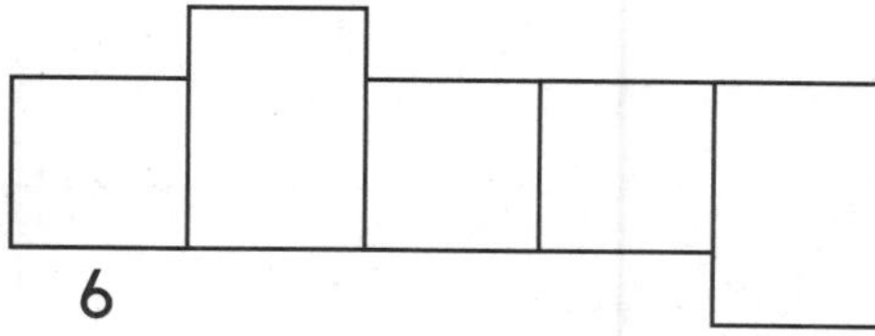

Write the letter with the number 1 under it on the first numbered line below. Do the same for numbers 2 through 6.

Riddle: Which part of a fish weighs the most?

Answer: the ___ ___ ___ ___ ___ ___
1 2 3 4 5 6

Spelling and Writing

Proofreading

Proofreading Marks

- (oval) spelling mistake
- ⊙ add period
- ℓ take out something

Each sentence has two mistakes. Use the proofreading marks to fix each mistake. Write the misspelled **list words** correctly on the lines.

1. A snaek and a turtle are alike because they are both reptiles.? 1. ______
2. Mose snakes and all turtles lay eggs 2. ______
3. When scared, a turtle will snap, but a snake will stryke with its fangs 3. ______

Making a Sign

Snakes are helpful animals. They eat bugs and other pests. Make a sign that asks people to be kind to snakes. Write your first draft on the lines. Then copy it onto another sheet of paper and add a picture.

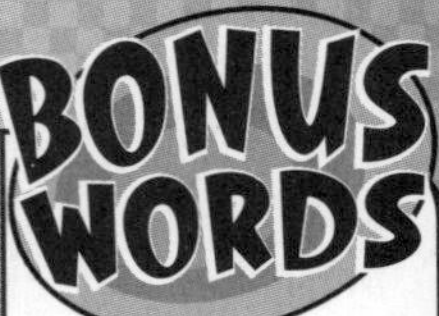

stream
splash
stamp
beast
sleepy

Spelling Words in Action

How can you tell the difference between a bone and a rock?

Dinosaur Dig

A paleontologist is someone who studies fossils. **Today**, Project Exploration helps **boys** and girls become Junior Paleontologists. **They** call themselves JPs for short. It **may** sound like fun to look for dinosaur bones. It can be a lot of hard work, too.

First the JPs train for two weeks. Then **they** travel far **away** from their homes.

The JPs go to the badlands of Montana. There they crawl on the ground. They use picks and paint brushes to search for tiny, **gray** fossils. They use their hands, eyes, brains, and even their tongues! Scientists **say** that one way to tell a bone from a rock is to lick it. If it sticks to your tongue, it is probably a bone.

Imagine the **joy** of finding a dinosaur fossil! Maybe someday you will not have to imagine it. You will really do it.

Look back at the words in dark print. The letter y with a, e, or o can spell vowel sounds. Say each word. What vowel sounds do you hear?

Spelling Practice

TIP

The letter **y** can team up with **a**, **e**, or **o** to spell vowel sounds. The long **a** sound can be spelled **ay**, as in say, or **ey**, as in they. The **oi** sound can also be spelled **oy**, as in joy.

LIST WORDS

1. plays
2. say
3. may
4. tray
5. gray
6. today
7. away
8. they
9. boys
10. joy

Spelling Vowel Sounds with y

Write each **list word** under the heading that shows the vowel sound **y** spells.

oy spells **oi**

1. ______________ 2. ______________

ay spells long **a**

3. ______________ 4. ______________

5. ______________ 6. ______________

7. ______________ 8. ______________

9. ______________

ey spells long **a**

10. ______________

Word Clues

Write the **list word** that matches each clue.

1. on this day, now

2. is allowed to

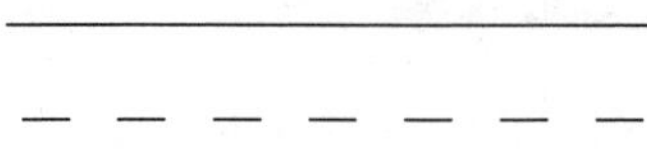

3. great happiness

4. not here

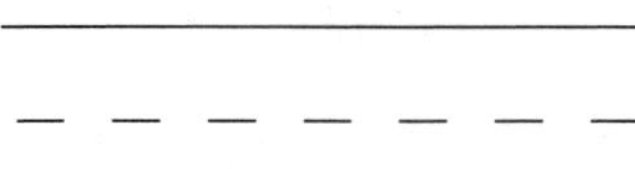

Word Puzzle

Read each clue. Write **list words** to fill in the puzzle.

Across

2. has fun
4. two or more
5. young men
7. a happy feeling

Down

1. a color
3. not here
4. something used to carry things
6. speak

Spelling and Writing

Proofreading

Proofreading Marks

- (oval) spelling mistakes
- (triple underline) capital letter
- (circled dot) add period

Each sentence has two mistakes. Use the proofreading marks to fix each mistake. Write the misspelled **list words** correctly on the lines.

1. project Exploration helps boyz and girls become Junior Paleontologists. 1. ________

2. They go awey to look for dinosaur fossils 2. ________

3. You meye find a dinosaur fossil someday, too 3. ________

Writing a Journal Entry

Pretend that you have just discovered an unusual dinosaur fossil. Write a journal entry telling how you felt about your discovery. Proofread your paragraph. Fix any mistakes.

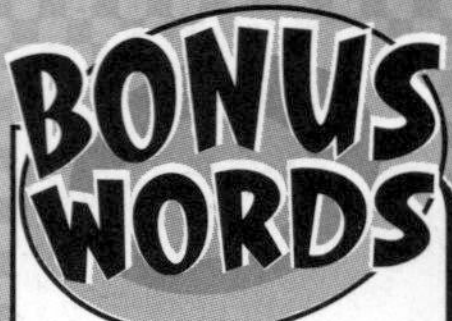

always
enjoy
holiday
Monday
stray

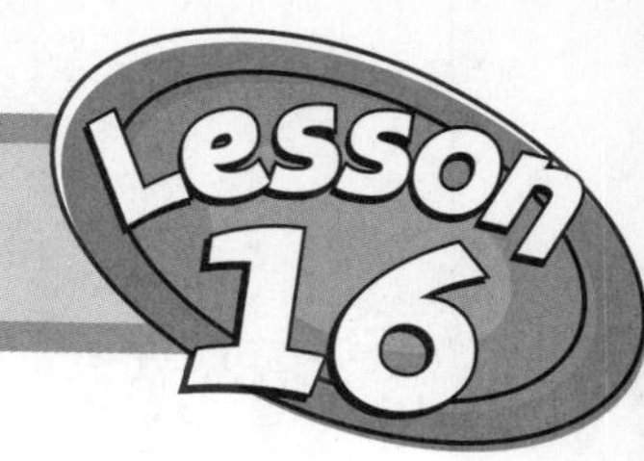

Spelling Words in Action

How does a flying fish fly?

A Fish Out of Water

You have probably seen birds and bugs fly **many** times. Did you know that some fish can fly? They are called flying fish.

Flying fish do not fly the same way as a bird or a bug. It **only** looks as if they do. Flying fish have fins shaped like wings. The fish swim very fast just below the surface of the water. Then they wiggle their tails. **By** wiggling their tails very fast, they are able to jump high out of the water. They sail through the air with their fins held out like wings. That is **why** it looks as if they are flying.

The trip lasts only a few seconds, but these **tiny** fish are fast. They can fly up to 30 miles an hour. Some can fly 1,000 feet in just one jump!

Say each word in dark print in the paragraphs. What vowel sound does the y stand for in each word?

Spelling Practice

TIP

The letter **y** can team up with **a**, **e**, or **o** to spell vowel sounds. It can also spell vowel sounds all by itself, such as the long **e** sound in many and the long **i** sound in fry.

LIST WORDS

1. bunny
2. many
3. fry
4. only
5. lucky
6. by
7. tiny
8. penny
9. why
10. key

Identifying y as a Vowel

Write each **list word** under the heading that shows its long vowel sound.

Long **e** sound

1. ____________ 2. ____________

3. ____________ 4. ____________

5. ____________ 6. ____________

7. ____________

Long **i** sound

8. ____________ 9. ____________

10. ____________

Read each clue. Write the **list word** that rhymes.

1. It's a way to cook.
   It rhymes with my.

2. This unlocks a door.
   It rhymes with me.

3. It can start a question.
   It rhymes with tie.

4. This means very small.
   It rhymes with shiny.

Dictionary

In the dictionary, the **sound spelling** shows how many syllables a word has.

story (stôr ē)

Write the **list words** that have one syllable.

1. ______ 2. ______
3. ______ 4. ______

Write the **list words** that have two syllables.

5. ______ 6. ______ 7. ______
8. ______ 9. ______ 10. ______

Spelling and Writing

Proofreading

Proofreading Marks

- spelling mistake (circle)
- add period (⊙)
- take out something

Each sentence has two mistakes. Use the proofreading marks to fix each mistake. Write the misspelled **list words** correctly on the lines.

1. The flying fish is not the onelee strange sea animal

2. The sea horse looks like a tinee horse.?

3. The electric eel has shocked menny people

1. ____________

2. ____________

3. ____________

Writing a Description

There are many different kinds of fish. Write a description of a fish you have seen or heard about. Proofread your description. Fix any mistakes.

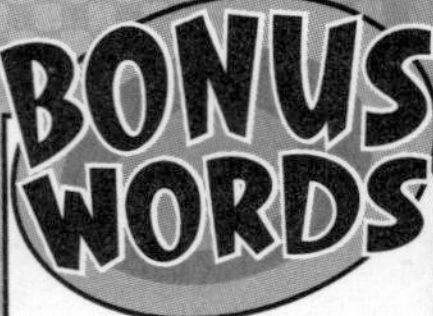

canary
shy
greedy
cherry
satisfy

Words with le

Spelling Words in Action

What kind of seeds did John Chapman plant?

America's Apple Man

Have you ever heard of John Chapman? In the 1800s he walked thousands of miles through many states. As he walked, he planted **apple** seeds.

People began to call him Johnny Appleseed. He wore old clothes and an old pot for a hat. When he was ready to cook, he grabbed the **handle** of the pot, took it off his head, and put it on the fire!

He was kind to wild animals and was **able** to get very close to them. Most of all, Johnny loved his apple trees. The next time you bite into an apple or see a **bottle** of apple juice, think of Johnny Appleseed. Some of the apple trees he planted so long ago are still growing.

Look back at the words in dark print. Say each word. What sound does le make at the end of each word?

Spelling Practice

TIP

Words with the **le** spelling at the end always have at least two syllables, as in **apple**. Listen for the sound **le** makes at the end of each **list word**.

LIST WORDS

1. apple *apple*
2. handle *handle*
3. able *able*
4. bottle *bottle*
5. table *table*
6. uncle *uncle*
7. candle *candle*
8. purple *purple*
9. turtle *turtle*
10. people *people*

Identifying le Endings

Write each **list word** under the heading that shows its second syllable.

ble

1. ______________ 2. ______________

tle

3. ______________ 4. ______________

cle

5. ______________

ple

6. ______________ 7. ______________

8. ______________

dle

9. ______________ 10. ______________

Alphabetical Order

Write these **list words** in alphabetical order.

handle apple bottle table people

1. ____________
2. ____________
3. ____________
4. ____________
5. ____________

Mixed Up Words

The underlined **list word** in each sentence does not make sense. Write the **list word** that does make sense on the line.

1. I have a pet apple. ____________
2. I like to bite into a nice red table. ____________
3. Hold the pan by its uncle. ____________
4. My favorite color is able. ____________
5. There was one turtle on the birthday cake. ____________
6. I put the cake on the candle. ____________

Spelling and Writing

Proofreading

Proofreading Marks

- (oval) spelling mistake
- ≡ capital letter
- ⊙ add period

Each sentence has two mistakes. Use the proofreading marks to fix each mistake. Write the misspelled **list words** on the lines.

1. an appel a day keeps the doctor away. 1. ______
2. My uncal says that may be true 2. ______
3. He is not a doctor, but he knows what is good for pepol 3. ______

Writing a Description

What other kinds of fruits grow on trees? Write a description of your favorite fruit that grows on a tree. Now proofread your description. Fix any mistakes.

______

______

______

nibble
eagle
gentle
tumble
sparkle

Lessons 13–17 • Review

In Lessons 13–17 you learned how to spell words with consonant blends **r**, **l**, and **s**, **y** with a vowel and **y** as a vowel, and words with **le** at the end.

Check Your Spelling Notebook

Look at the words in your spelling notebook. Which words in Lessons 13 through 17 did you have the most trouble with? Write them here.

____

Lesson 13

In a blend, you can hear each of the consonants that go together. Listen for the l blend in <u>flew</u> and the r blend in <u>truck</u>.

List Words

- class
- from
- friend
- glove

Write the **list word** that rhymes.

1. love ____________ 2. glass ____________

3. send ____________ 4. drum ____________

Lesson 14

TIP **The letter s can work with two or more letters to make a blend at the beginning or the end of a word. Listen for the s blends in the words smell and most.**

List Words

slice
smoke
spell
swim

Write the **list word** that belongs in each group.

1. pool, water,

2. letters, words,

3. fire, chimney,

4. pizza, pie,

Lesson 15

The letter y with a vowel can have the long a sound, as in say or they. It can also have the oi sound, as in joy.

List Words

boys
they
joy
today

Write the **list word** that matches each clue.

1. This is great happiness.

2. She and he together.

3. These are young men.

4. This day is now.

Lesson 16

TIP **The letter y by itself can spell vowel sounds like the long e sound in only and the long i sound in fry.**

List Words

by
tiny
key
why

Write a **list word** to finish each sentence.

1. The baby kitten is so ______________.
2. I walked home all ______________ myself.
3. I don't know ______________ she was late.
4. This ______________ unlocks the front door.

Lesson 17

TIP **The le sound always adds another syllable to a word, as in handle.**

List Words

candle
apple
table
turtle

Write a **list word** to match each clue.

1. an animal ______________
2. a fruit ______________
3. a light ______________
4. a piece of furniture ______________

Show What You Know

Lessons 13–17 Review

One word is misspelled in each set of **list words**. Fill in the circle next to the **list word** that is spelled incorrectly.

1.	○ plays	○ tiney	○ uncle	○ only
2.	○ flew	○ many	○ sae	○ swim
3.	○ why	○ playt	○ table	○ trunk
4.	○ peeple	○ joy	○ snake	○ penny
5.	○ able	○ smell	○ grass	○ smok
6.	○ flat	○ buny	○ may	○ truck
7.	○ story	○ key	○ purple	○ gluv
8.	○ bottle	○ today	○ flat	○ mosht
9.	○ gray	○ by	○ thay	○ from
10.	○ spell	○ appel	○ friend	○ lucky
11.	○ ownlee	○ fry	○ people	○ class
12.	○ chruck	○ handle	○ away	○ say
13.	○ glove	○ slice	○ turtle	○ joi
14.	○ candle	○ boys	○ tabl	○ bunny
15.	○ they	○ tray	○ smeell	○ strike
16.	○ still	○ apple	○ uncle	○ gra
17.	○ most	○ kee	○ by	○ flew
18.	○ frend	○ swim	○ class	○ tiny
19.	○ away	○ snake	○ plate	○ botle
20.	○ grass	○ smoke	○ menny	○ purple

Words with sh and th

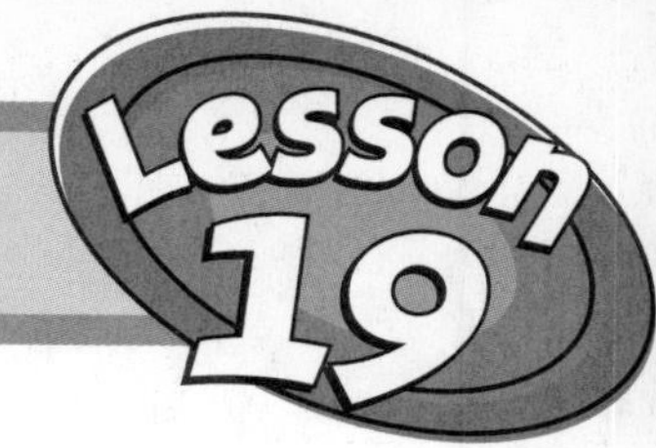

Spelling Words in Action

What did people do before they had TV?

See with Your Ears!

Three actors stand **together** in a studio. One man begins to **shout**, "**Shut** the door! I'm freezing!"

Crash! You can hear the sound of a door slamming, but there is no door to see. These actors are performing on the radio.

Today, many people listen to music on the radio. Fifty years ago, people listened to stories. There was no TV back **then**.

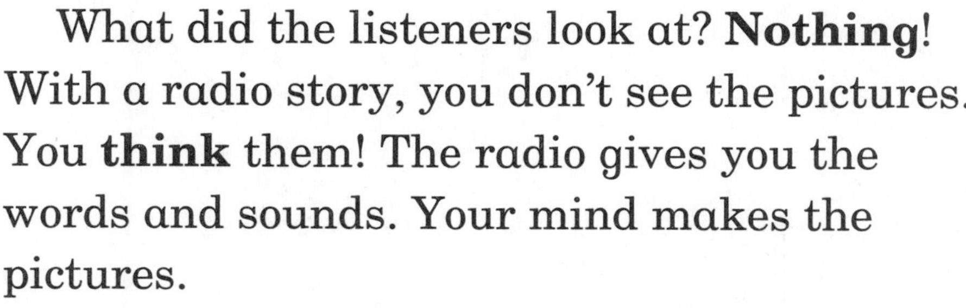

What did the listeners look at? **Nothing**! With a radio story, you don't see the pictures. You **think** them! The radio gives you the words and sounds. Your mind makes the pictures.

Did you know you can still hear radio stories? Why not tune in and listen?

Look back at the words in dark print. Say each word. How many consonant sounds do you hear at the beginning of the words?

Spelling Practice

When two consonants make one sound it is called a **consonant digraph**. Listen for the sound **th** makes in think and then. Listen for the sound **sh** makes in shut and shout.

LIST WORDS

1. shout *shout*
2. shut *shut*
3. crash *crash*
4. then *then*
5. thin *thin*
6. math *math*
7. think *think*
8. together *together*
9. nothing *nothing*
10. anything *anything*

Adding Consonant Digraphs

Add a consonant digraph to each group of letters to make a word. Trace the letters to spell **list words**.

1. ____ink
2. ____out
3. ma____
4. toge____er
5. any____ing
6. cra____
7. no____ing
8. ____en
9. ____ut
10. ____in

Opposites

Write the **list word** that means the opposite of the word or words.

1. thick ______________________ 2. whisper ______________________

3. open ______________________ 4. everything ______________________

5. alone ______________________ 6. now ______________________

7. a special thing ______________________

Word Search

There are four **list words** in the puzzle. They may go across or down. Circle each word. Then, write the words on the lines.

1. ______________________

2. ______________________

3. ______________________

4. ______________________

B	C	E	I	P	M	Q
G	A	T	S	T	A	L
O	S	H	O	U	T	B
Z	J	I	F	D	H	C
K	G	N	O	T	D	A
D	B	K	L	I	X	M
A	C	R	A	S	H	S

Spelling and Writing

Proofreading

Proofreading Marks

 spelling mistake
capital letter
take out something

Each sentence has two mistakes. Use the proofreading marks to fix each mistake. Write the misspelled **list words** correctly on the lines.

1. I thenk radio shows are are fun. 1. ______
2. My brother and i listen to the radio tugethr. 2. ______
3. we shet our eyes and imagine what is happening. 3. ______

Writing a Radio Play

What kind of radio story would you like to write? Write a sentence to tell what the story would be about. Write one or two sentences that actors will say in your play. Describe the sounds, too.

______

______

______

BONUS WORDS

shell
gather
shape
shore
thick

Spelling Words in Action

What is a galago?

Night Jumper

Some animals have **such** funny names. One is the galago.

Galagos live in Africa **where** there are many trees. Galagos live in trees. Their long hind legs help them jump from branch to branch. Galagos can jump as far as 15 feet.

Galagos sleep during the day. They are active **when** it is night. Their large eyes help them see well in the dark.

Galagos can be as big as a squirrel or as small as a chipmunk. They have soft fur and a long tail. They have fingers and toes that help them hold on to things.

What an interesting animal a galago is. They are so **much** fun to watch. **Who** would not want to see one? The next time you visit a zoo, see if there is a galago living there.

Look back at the words in dark print. Say each word. What sound do the consonants wh and ch stand for in each word?

Spelling Practice

A **consonant digraph** is two consonants that make one sound. The letters **ch** spell one sound, as in such. The letters **wh** spell the sound you hear in what.

LIST WORDS

1. what *what*
2. such *such*
3. where *where*
4. peach *peach*
5. much *much*
6. when *when*
7. whip *whip*
8. arch *arch*
9. coach *coach*
10. who *who*

Identifying Consonant Digraphs

Write each **list word** under the heading that shows its consonant digraph.

ch

1. ______________ 2. ______________

3. ______________ 4. ______________

5. ______________

wh

6. ______________ 7. ______________

8. ______________ 9. ______________

10. ______________

Word Meaning

Write the **list word** that matches each meaning.

1. A lot ____________
2. A kind of fruit ____________
3. What people? ____________
4. Leader of a team ____________
5. What time? ____________
6. What place? ____________

Rhyming Clues

Write **list words** that rhyme with the clues.

1. This word rhymes with <u>there</u>. ____________
2. This word rhymes with <u>ship</u>. ____________
3. This word rhymes with <u>march</u>. ____________
4. This word rhymes with <u>mutt</u>. ____________
5. These two words rhyme with each other. ____________ ____________

Spelling and Writing

Proofreading

The paragraph below has six mistakes. Use the proofreading marks to fix each mistake. Write the misspelled **list words** correctly on the lines.

Proofreading Marks

- ⬭ spelling mistake
- ⊙ add period
- ^ add something

Have you ever seen an unusual looking animal Whut did it look like? Was it cute? Was it funny looking Wheen you go for a walk, look around. See how many animals you can find. Make a list that tells what they look like Share your list with your friends. See how mech they know about the animals you saw.

1. ______________
2. ______________
3. ______________

Writing a Description

What is your favorite animal? What does it look like? Why is it your favorite? Write sentences to describe your favorite animal. Proofread your description. Fix any mistakes.

____

____

BONUS WORDS

- child
- whale
- wheat
- sandwich
- cheese

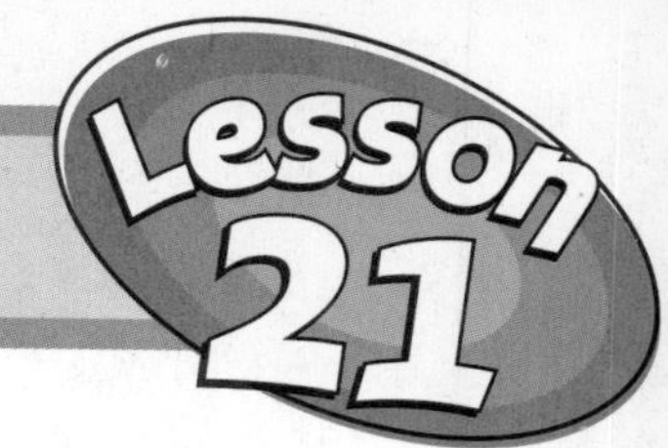

Spelling Words in Action

What kind of sock does not go on your foot?

How to Make a Wind Sock

A wind sock is a tube of fabric that hangs on a pole or **stick**. When the wind blows, the tube fills with air. By looking at the wind sock you can tell which way the wind is blowing.

A wind sock is **quick** and easy to make. It might cost more than one **cent**, but it will not cost very much. Use a piece of cloth about two feet wide and three feet long. Use markers or paint to **color** a design on the **back**. Next, sew the long edges of the cloth together to make a tube. Then, bend thin metal or a wire coat hanger into the shape of a circle. Sew one end of the tube onto the hoop. Attach some string and tie your wind sock to a stick. Now, wait for the wind to blow!

Look back at the words in dark print. Say each word. Which word begins with c, but has the s sound? In which words can you hear the k sound?

Spelling Practice

The letter **c** can make the **k** sound, as in color, or the **s** sound, as in race. When the letters **c** and **k** come together, they make the **k** sound, as in kick.

LIST WORDS

1. race *race*
2. stick *stick*
3. color *color*
4. kick *kick*
5. quick *quick*
6. back *back*
7. became *became*
8. neck *neck*
9. cent *cent*
10. city *city*

Showing the Sound c Makes

Write each **list word** under the heading that shows the sound **c** spells.

c spells **s**

1. ________________ 2. ________________

3. ________________

ck spells **k**

4. ________________ 5. ________________

6. ________________ 7. ________________

8. ________________

c spells **k**

9. ________________ 10. ________________

Word Groups

Write the **list word** that belongs with each group.

1. head, shoulders,

   ____

2. hit, strike,

   ____

3. dime, nickel,

   ____

4. town, village,

   ____

5. fast, swift,

   ____

6. twig, pole,

   ____

Story

Write **list words** to finish the story.

The Big Race

I am going to run in a __________ today. The ____________ of my team's shirts is red. We ____________________ known as the Red Racers. Each runner has to run to a tree and ___________ , carrying a stick. Then, the runner passes the ___________ to the next runner. This kind of race is called a relay race.

Spelling and Writing

Proofreading

Proofreading Marks

- ⬭ spelling mistake
- ⊙ add period
- ℓ take something out

Each sentence has two mistakes. Use the proofreading marks to fix each mistake. Write the misspelled **list words** correctly on the lines.

1. Our team won the the rase today! 1. ____________

2. We were quik on the track 2. ____________

3. Next week, we'll ride to the cite to race a new team 3. ____________

Writing Directions

Have you ever made a wind sock, a pinwheel, or a paper airplane? Write sentences that tell how to make something.

____

____

____

BONUS WORDS

- camera
- coconut
- space
- pack
- circle

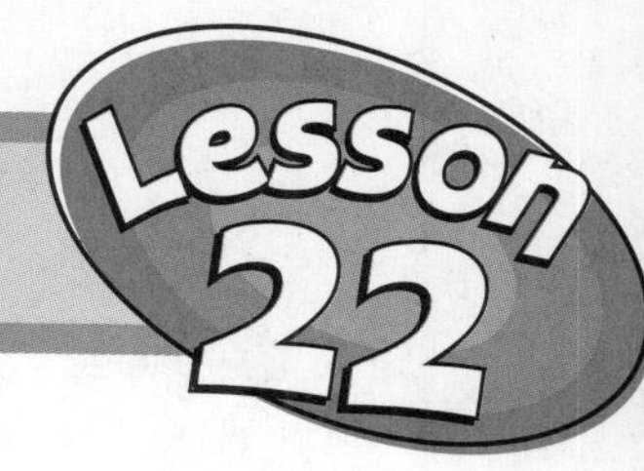

Spelling Words in Action

What is a fun way to learn about another country?

A Far Away Place

One girl lives on a **farm** in Iowa. Another girl lives in a big city **far** away in Japan. How can they be friends? They are pen pals.

Pen pals are friends who write letters to each other. Many groups help school children find pen pals in other countries.

The girl in Iowa might tell her pen pal about the **corn** her family grows on their farm. She might tell about the farm animals, a **horse** or a cow. She might write about what it's like at her school.

Her pen pal can tell her what things are like in Japan. They can each learn **more** about each others' country. It's not **hard** at all. It's fun!

Say each word in dark print in the paragraphs. What sounds do ar and or spell?

Spelling Practice

When a vowel is followed by **r**, the vowel sound is changed by the **r**. Listen for the **or** sound in corn and the **ar** sound in farm.

LIST WORDS

1. farm *farm*
2. corn *corn*
3. hard *hard*
4. park *park*
5. part *part*
6. horse *horse*
7. more *more*
8. far *far*
9. floor *floor*
10. warm *warm*

Adding or and ar

Add **ar** or **or** to make **list words**. Trace the letters to spell **list words**.

1. m e
2. p k
3. w m
4. c n
5. h d
6. flo
7. p t
8. f m
9. f
10. h se

Opposites

Write the **list word** that means the opposite.

1. near ______________________ 2. soft ______________________

3. less ______________________ 4. cool ______________________

5. ceiling ______________________ 6. whole ______________________

Word Puzzle

Read each clue. Write **list words** to fill in the puzzle.

Across

2. a place to play
3. where animals or crops are grown
4. a kind of vegetable
5. an animal you ride
6. not nearby

Down

1. not cold
3. what you walk on
5. not soft

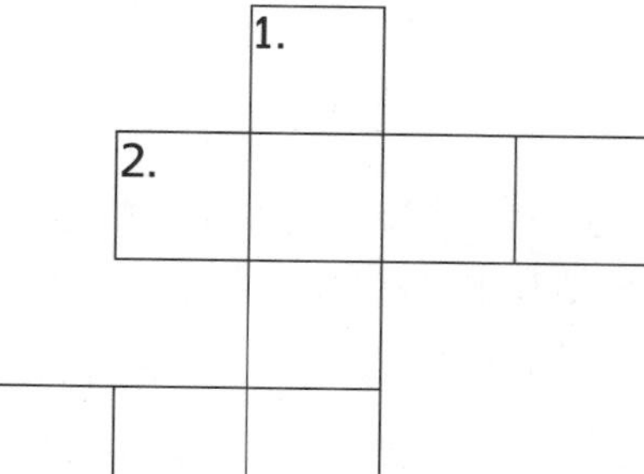

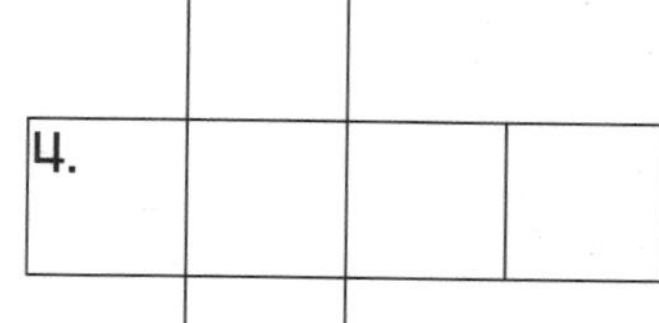

6.

Spelling and Writing

Proofreading

Each sentence has two mistakes. Use the proofreading marks to fix each mistake. Write the misspelled **list words** correctly on the lines.

Proofreading Marks

- ⬭ spelling mistake
- ≡ capital letter
- ^ add something

1. Jerry visited his aunt's faerm in idaho. 1. ______________

2. Aunt jessie worked haard all day. 2. ______________

3. What parte of the farm do you like best 3. ______________

Writing a Letter

Imagine you have a pen pal in another country. Write a letter to your pen pal.

____

____

____

____

____

start

born

cart

forest

alarm

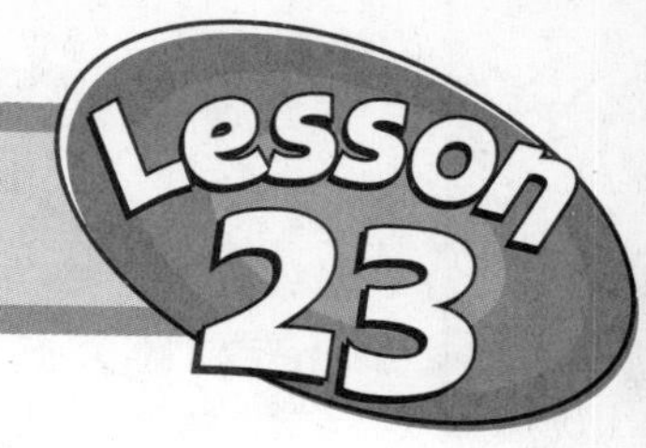

Spelling Words in Action

Do you know what a spelling shortcut is?

Spelling Shortcuts

In this lesson, **you'll** be spelling some shortcut words. **They're** called contractions. You already say many contractions every day. **It's** an easy way to talk.

Contractions join two words into one. You might say, "**We're** going to the park." We're is a contraction. It is a short way of writing "we are."

This mark (') takes the place of the letter or letters you took away. This little mark has a big name. It's called an apostrophe. Use it to combine two words into one shorter word. **Isn't** that easy?

Let's see if you can find all the contractions in this story. It isn't hard to do. They're easy to see, **aren't** they? Just look for that little mark. **I'm** sure you can do it. You just **can't** miss!

Look back at the words in dark print. Say each word. What two words make up the contraction? What letter or letters does the apostrophe replace?

Spelling Practice

TIP

A **contraction** is two words combined into one. One or more letters are dropped. A mark called an **apostrophe** (') replaces the missing letters.

LIST WORDS

1. you'll *you'll*
2. they're *they're*
3. it's *it's*
4. we've *we've*
5. isn't *isn't*
6. let's *let's*
7. aren't *aren't*
8. I'm *I'm*
9. can't *can't*
10. we're *we're*

Adding Apostrophes

The apostrophe (') is missing from each **list word** below. Write the correct **list word** on the line. Put the apostrophe in the right place.

1. youll ____________________
2. lets ____________________
3. cant ____________________
4. Im ____________________
5. were ____________________
6. its ____________________
7. theyre ____________________
8. isnt ____________________
9. arent ____________________
10. were ____________________

Word Addition

Write the **list word** that solves each "addition" problem.

1. let + us = ____________
2. they + are = ____________
3. we + have = ____________
4. we + are = ____________
5. can + not = ____________
6. is + not = ____________
7. are + not = ____________
8. it + is = ____________
9. I + am = ____________
10. you + will = ____________

Rhyming Clues

Read each clue. Write a **list word** that rhymes on the line.

1. I am a contraction that rhymes with time.

____

2. Let us print a word that rhymes with gets.

____

3. We have a word that rhymes with sleeve.

____

4. It is a word that rhymes with bits.

____

Spelling and Writing

Proofreading

Each sentence has two mistakes. Use the proofreading marks to fix each mistake. Write the **list words** correctly on the lines.

Proofreading Marks

- add apostrophe
- capital letter
- add period

1. On the Fourth of July, youll see many families in the parks 1. ____________
2. usually, theyre eating or playing games. 2. ____________
3. Its a day for singing the "Star spangled Banner." 3. ____________

Writing a Description

A contraction is a kind of shortcut. Shortcuts save time. Write a description of a shortcut you know at home or at school.

____

____

____

____

doesn't
I'd
weren't
you've
mustn't

Lessons 19–23 • Review

In Lessons 19–23 you learned how to spell words with consonant digraphs and words with vowels and the letter **r**. You also learned the sounds that **c** and **ck** can make and how to write contractions.

Check Your Spelling Notebook

Look at the words in your spelling notebook. Which words for Lessons 19 through 23 did you have the most trouble with? Write them here.

____

____

Lesson 19

Some consonant pairs spell one sound. They are called consonant digraphs. Listen for the sh sound, as in crash, and the th sound, as in then.

List Words

nothing
shout
shut
thin

Write the **list word** that means the same or almost the same as each word.

1. skinny ____________ 2. yell ____________

3. zero ____________ 4. close ____________

Lesson 20

TIP **The letter pairs ch and wh are consonant digraphs. Listen for the ch sound, as in coach, and the wh sound, as in whip.**

Write a **list word** to finish each sentence.

List Words

- much
- peach
- when
- where

1. ______________ will the movie begin?

2. ______________ do you live?

3. How ______________ does it cost?

4. May I eat the ______________?

Lesson 21

TIP **You can hear the k sound with the letter c in became. The letter c can also make the s sound, as in cent. When the letters c and k come together, you hear the k sound, as in neck.**

Write each **list word** next to its dictionary sound-spelling.

List Words

- cent
- race
- color
- stick

1. (kul′ ər) ______________ 2. (rās) ______________

3. (stik) ______________ 4. (sent) ______________

Lesson 22

TIP **When r follows a vowel, it changes the vowel sound. Listen for the or sound, as in corn, and the ar sound, as in farm.**

List Words

floor
more
hard
warm

Write the **list word** that finishes each sentence.

1. Stand in the ______________ sunshine.

2. I'd like ______________ milk, please.

3. This problem is ______________.

4. Mop the ______________.

Lesson 23

A contraction is made by combining two words and dropping one or more letters. An apostrophe (') replaces the missing letters, as in they're.

List Words

isn't
we're
let's
you'll

Write the **list word** that means the same.

1. you will ______________ 2. we are ______________

3. let us ______________ 4. is not ______________

Show What You Know

Lessons 19–23 Review

One word is misspelled in each set of **list words**. Fill in the circle next to the **list word** that is spelled incorrectly.

1.	○ think	○ citie	○ such	○ floor
2.	○ cann't	○ far	○ kick	○ what
3.	○ became	○ much	○ corn	○ togeter
4.	○ cent	○ let's	○ parc	○ where
5.	○ thin	○ arche	○ hard	○ color
6.	○ moore	○ who	○ back	○ it's
7.	○ krash	○ farm	○ when	○ race
8.	○ coach	○ part	○ neck	○ you'l
9.	○ shut	○ whipp	○ quick	○ warm
10.	○ I'm	○ then	○ it's	○ stik
11.	○ anything	○ horse	○ isnn't	○ math
12.	○ they're	○ nothin	○ shout	○ who
13.	○ thin	○ back	○ peach	○ flore
14.	○ rase	○ hard	○ what	○ aren't
15.	○ peech	○ cent	○ then	○ we've
16.	○ it's	○ much	○ kick	○ schut
17.	○ such	○ color	○ farr	○ math
18.	○ when	○ quik	○ we're	○ corn
19.	○ neck	○ think	○ part	○ we'er
20.	○ arenn't	○ warm	○ coach	○ think

Vowels with r

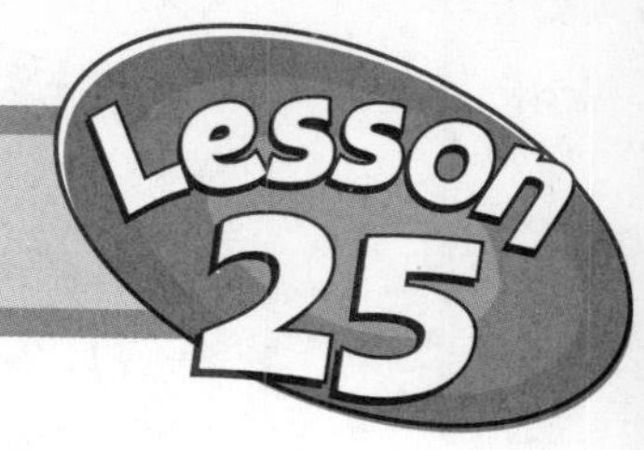

Spelling Words in Action

How much does a giant pumpkin weigh?

The Bigger the Better

Some people like to grow giant fruits and vegetables. They want to break **world** records.

A woman in Pennsylvania grew a pumpkin that weighed 1,131 pounds! **Her** pumpkin was really big.

In North Carolina, a man named Harry Hurley broke the biggest bean record for the **first** time in 1996. The bean was 4 feet long! One year later, he had another **turn** to break the world record. This time his giant bean was 4 feet 3 1/2 inches long.

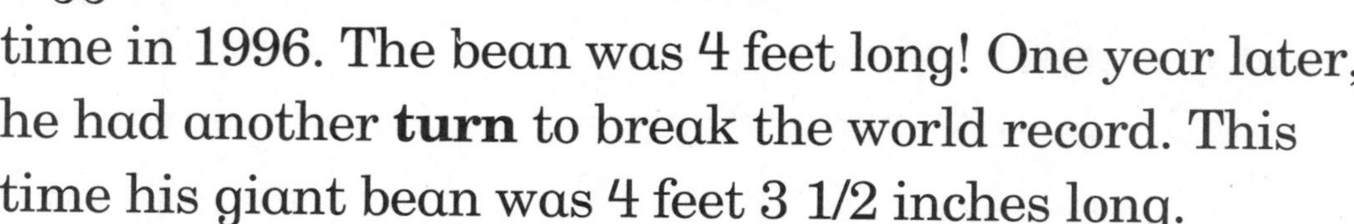

In 2000, a company in England grew the largest tomato plant in the world. It grew to be 65 feet tall! That was **worth** a world record, too. People **were** able to pick 1,000 tomatoes off the giant plant.

Look back at the words in dark print. Say each word. What vowel sounds do you hear?

Spelling Practice

TIP

When **r** follows the vowels **e**, **i**, **o**, or **u**, it can make the **ur** sound you hear in her and sir. That sound is spelled **er**, **ir**, **or**, or **ur**.

LIST WORDS

1. world *world*
2. girl *girl*
3. skirt *skirt*
4. her *her*
5. first *first*
6. worth *worth*
7. word *word*
8. sir *sir*
9. turn *turn*
10. were *were*

Adding Vowels with r

Add **er**, **ir**, **or**, or **ur** to each word to make a **list word**. Trace the letters to spell **list words**.

1. h____
2. g__l
3. w__e
4. w__ld
5. t__n
6. w__th
7. s__
8. sk__t
9. w__d
10. f__st

Word Clues

Write a **list word** to match each clue.

1. This is a young woman.

____

2. Earth is this.

____

3. You make this with letters.

____

4. This is a piece of clothing.

____

5. This comes before second.

____

6. You might call a man this.

____

Word Search

There are four **list words** in the puzzle. They may go across or down. Circle each word. Then write the words on the lines.

B	C	E	I	P	M	Q
G	W	O	R	T	H	L
O	E	H	O	U	E	B
Z	R	E	T	U	R	N
K	E	R	O	T	D	A
D	B	K	L	I	X	M

1. _______________

2. _______________

3. _______________

4. _______________

Spelling and Writing

Proofreading

Proofreading Marks

Mark	Meaning
⬭	spelling mistake
⊙	add period
^	add something

Each sentence has two mistakes. Use the proofreading marks to fix each mistake. Write the misspelled **list words** correctly on the lines.

1. The largest carrot in the worle weighed over 18 pounds 1. ______________

2. It was the furst carrot ever to grow that big 2. ______________

3. What do you think a carrot that size is werth 3. ______________

Writing an Ad

Write an ad for the world's biggest pizza. How big will it be? How many slices will it have? Proofread your ad and fix any mistakes.

____

____

____

BONUS WORDS

beaver
curtain
dirt
shirt
worm

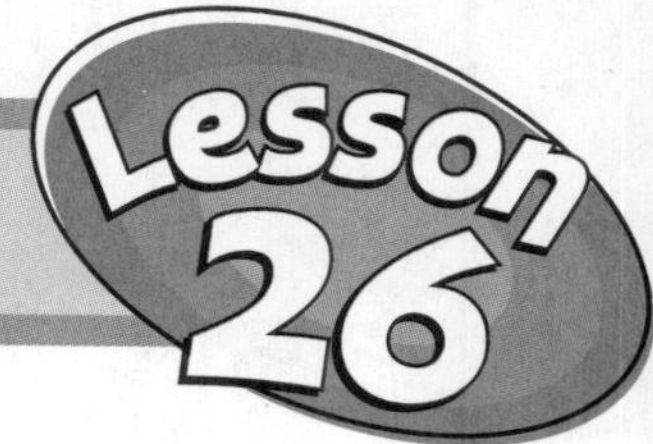

Spelling Words in Action

What does a lookout do?

Sky High

The U.S. Forest Service began **sending** people to live in lookout towers in the 1930s. These tall towers are usually built on top of mountains, so a lookout **sees** a long, long way.

Hundreds or even thousands of steps had to be climbed before a lookout **reached** the top of the tower. The small room at the top of the tower was where a lookout lived and **worked**.

Lookouts watched for signs of **burning** forest fires. They used field **glasses**, or binoculars, to help them. Then they'd call for help.

Nowadays there are not many jobs for lookouts. There are still many lookout towers, though. Some are rented to campers. If you think you would like to sleep hundreds of feet above the ground, a lookout tower might be for you.

Say each word in dark print in the paragraphs. How many different endings do you hear?

Spelling Practice

TIP

All of the **list words** have been built from base words and the endings **s** or **es**, **ed**, or **ing**. Add **es** to words that end in **x**, **s**, **sh**, or **ch**, such as wishes or boxes. Just add **s** to words ending in other letters, such as wants or sees.

LIST WORDS

1. worked *worked*
2. sending *sending*
3. wants *wants*
4. glasses *glasses*
5. sees *sees*
6. burning *burning*
7. reached *reached*
8. boxes *boxes*
9. wishes *wishes*
10. opening *opening*

Adding Endings

Add **s, es, ed,** or **ing** to each word to make a **list word**. Trace the letters to spell **list words**.

1. see ______
2. reach ______
3. want ______
4. wish ______
5. work ______
6. box ______
7. glass ______
8. burn ______
9. send ______
10. open ______

Word Meaning

Write the **list word** that matches each meaning.

1. uses the eyes ______________
2. wishes to have ______________
3. you drink from these ______________
4. a place to go through ______________
5. on fire ______________
6. mailing ______________

Scrambled Letters

Unscramble the letters to make **list words**. Then use the number code to answer the riddle.

1. esndgin

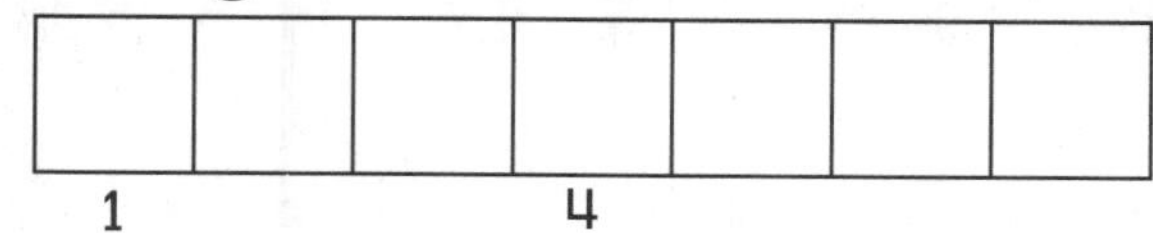

2. antws

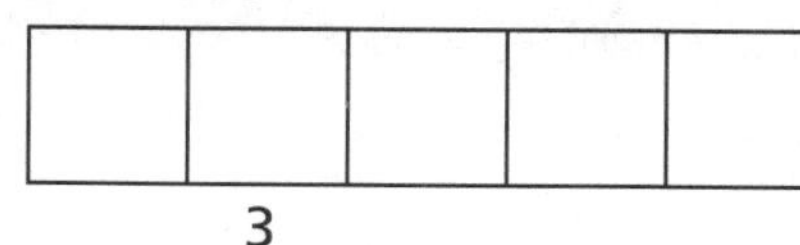

3. shiwes

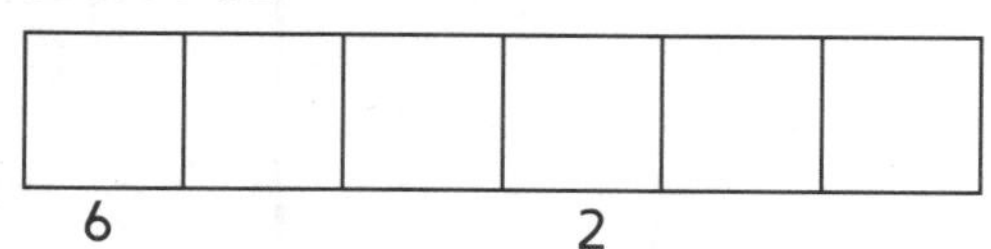

4. obxse

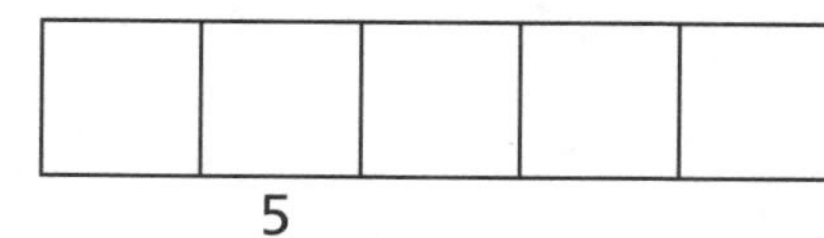

Find the letter with the number 1 under it. Write that letter on the line below that has the number 1 under it. Do the same for the numbers 2 through 6.

Riddle: What is dark but made by light?

Answer: ___ ___ ___ ___ ___ ___
1 2 3 4 5 6

Spelling and Writing

Proofreading

Each sentence has two mistakes. Use the proofreading marks to fix each mistake. Write the misspelled **list words** correctly on the lines.

Proofreading Marks

⬭	spelling mistake
≡	capital letter
⊙	add period

1. the firefighters workt hard to put out the fire. 1. ____________

2. The fire reachd the river 2. ____________

3. The firefighters were happy the fire had stopped burnning 3. ____________

Writing a Thank You Letter

For many years, Smokey the Bear has been helping to prevent forest fires. Write a letter to Smokey thanking him for doing such a great job.

____

____

____

____

pushed
marching
rushes
sweeps
crashes

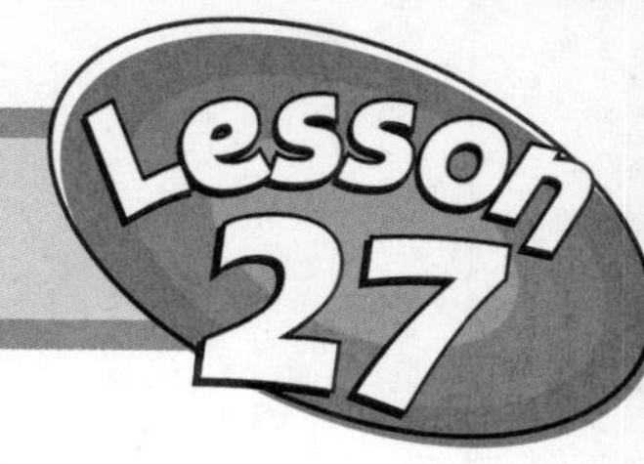

Spelling Words in Action

What are some different ways to jump rope?

It's as good for you as **jogging** or swimming. It's as fast as **running**. It can make your heart and lungs stronger. You can do it indoors or out, and it's a lot of fun. What is it? It's jumping rope.

There are many ways to jump rope. You can jump in place. You can try **skipping** forward or backward as you jump. Double Dutch is when two people spin the rope and two people jump at the same time.

There are many jump rope clubs around the country. Club members go to contests all over the country. They are **gladdest** when their team is **winning**. Even when they're not winning, though, they all love jumping rope.

Look back at the words in dark print. Say each word. What consonants are doubled to make each ending?

The final consonant in most short-vowel words is doubled when an ending is added. This rule works for most of the list words:
jog + ing = jogging

LIST WORDS

1. jogging *jogging*
2. running *running*
3. trimming *trimming*
4. skipping *skipping*
5. shopped *shopped*
6. sadder *sadder*
7. gladdest *gladdest*
8. hopped *hopped*
9. winning *winning*
10. mixed *mixed*

Spelling Practice

Adding Endings

Add **ed, ing, er,** or **est** to each base word to make a **list word**. Double the final consonant of all words except one. Trace the letters to spell **list words**.

1. shop ______
2. trim ______
3. skip ______
4. mix ______
5. win ______
6. sad ______
7. hop ______
8. run ______
9. glad ______
10. jog ______

Word Groups

Write the **list word** that belongs with each group.

1. cutting, clipping, ______________________
2. looked at, paid for, ______________________
3. getting, earning, ______________________
4. stirred, blended, ______________________
5. most joyful, happiest, ______________________
6. running, skipping, ______________________

Word Puzzle

Read each clue. Write **list words** to fill in the puzzle.

Across

1. more unhappy
3. stirred together
5. jumped up and down on one foot

Down

1. hopping along from one foot to the other
2. faster than walking or jogging
4. a little faster than walking

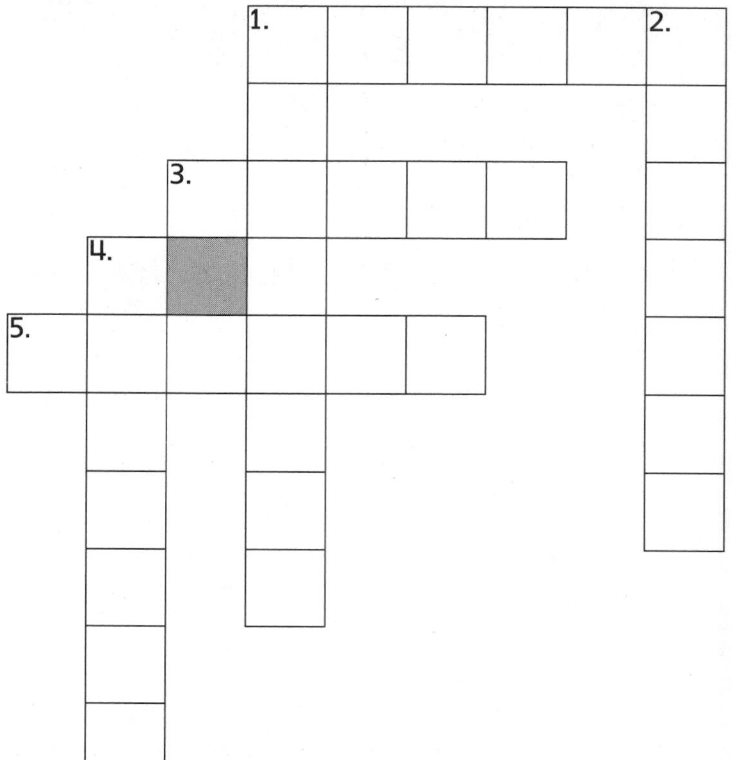

Spelling and Writing

Proofreading

Proofreading Marks

	spelling mistake
⊙	add period
❛	add apostrophe

Each sentence has two mistakes. Use the proofreading marks to fix each mistake. Write the misspelled **list words** correctly on the lines.

1. Some people like joging, because its good exercise. 1. ____________________
2. Other people like ronning because they go faster 2. ____________________
3. Wining a race isnt important, but staying healthy is. 3. ____________________

Writing a Rhyme

"One, two, buckle my shoe. Three, four, shut the door." Jump rope rhymes are fun. Write your own jump rope rhyme. Proofread your rhyme and fix any mistakes.

____

____

____

BONUS WORDS

thinnest
napped
madder
begged
hugging

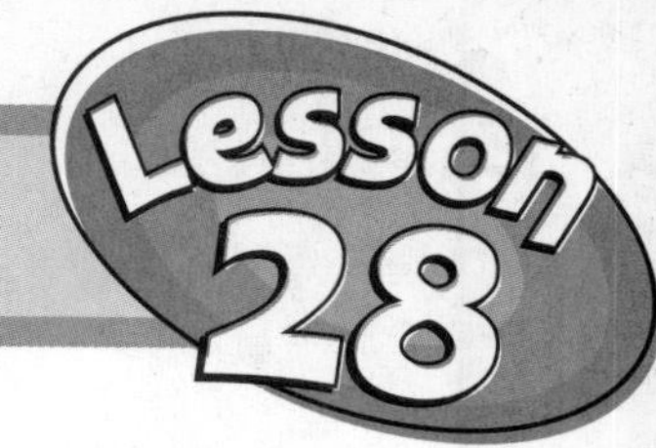

Spelling Words in Action

What is your favorite way to eat potatoes?

Are You a Potato-Head?

If you like to eat potatoes, you are not alone. The average American **loves** them. Every day, fast-food places are **serving** millions of pounds of french fries, **fried** potatoes. Maybe you will be **having** potatoes with your dinner tonight. They may be fried, **baked**, or mashed.

Potatoes are not only good to eat. They are good for you. They contain lots of Vitamin C. Our **bodies** need Vitamin C to help us grow strong and healthy.

Potatoes are not just for eating, though. One of the **funniest** ways potatoes are used is in Shelley, Idaho. This town holds an annual festival with a mashed potato tug-of-war. Instead of mud, the loser gets pulled through a giant pile of mashed potatoes!

Look at each word in dark print. What do you notice about the spelling of the base word when the ending is added?

When a word ends in silent **e**, drop the **e** to add endings that begin with a vowel, such as **es**, **ed**, or **ing**.

have + ing = having

bake + ed = baked

When a word ends in **y** after a consonant, change **y** to **i** to add the endings **ed**, **es**, **er**, and **est**.

lucky + er = luckier

LIST WORDS

1. having *having*
2. serving *serving*
3. loves *loves*
4. baked *baked*
5. trades *trades*
6. fried *fried*
7. bodies *bodies*
8. luckier *luckier*
9. funniest *funniest*
10. carries *carries*

Spelling Practice

Adding Endings

The headings tell which ending made the **list word**. Write each **list word** under the right heading.

added **s**

1. ______________ 2. ______________

dropped final **e**

3. ______________ 4. ______________

5. ______________

changed **y** to **i**

6. ______________ 7. ______________

8. ______________ 9. ______________

10. ______________

Word Clues

Write **list words** to match each clue.

1. People exercise to keep these fit.

____

2. The waitress is doing this to our lunch.

____

3. This describes someone who tells the best jokes.

____

4. Matt does this with his baseball cards.

____

5. The cook did this to make a cake.

____

6. When more good things happen to you, you are this.

____

7. The mailman does this with letters he brings.

____

8. When you are eating, you are doing this to a meal.

____

Rhyming

Write a **list word** that rhymes with the underlined word.

1. It is a way to cook. It rhymes with <u>tried</u>.

____

2. This is a way of feeling. It rhymes with <u>doves</u>.

____

Spelling and Writing

Proofreading

Each sentence has two mistakes. Use the proofreading marks to fix each mistake. Write the misspelled **list words** correctly on the lines.

Proofreading Marks

- ⬭ spelling mistake
- ^ add something
- ⊙ add period

1. Are you haveing three balanced meals a day

2. You should eat one serveing of fruit or vegetables with every meal

3. Remember, healthy bodys need healthy food

1. ________________

2. ________________

3. ________________

Writing a Recipe

What is your favorite food? Write sentences that tell about your favorite food and how to make it.

____

____

____

____

BONUS WORDS

- healthier
- sleepiest
- tired
- palest
- blueberries

Words with Vowel Pairs

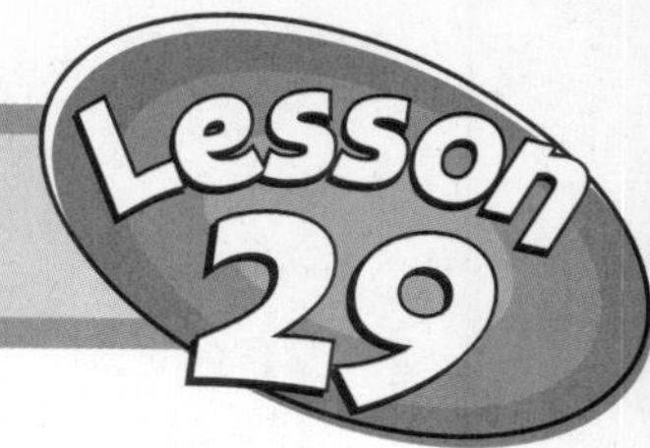

Spelling Words in Action

Where do frogs live?

Creature Feature

They have bulging eyes and long back legs. They live on land and in water. They catch bugs with their tongues. They **lay** eggs. What are they? They're frogs!

Frogs vary in color and size. The **main** colors are green or brown. Cricket frogs are only 1/2 inch long. Bullfrogs can grow to be 8 inches long. The biggest is the Goliath frog in Africa. It can be one foot long.

Tree frogs live on the **lower** branches of trees near ponds and streams. Suction pads on their **toes** help them climb trees.

Read about frogs in your area. Then the next time you're near a pond or stream, see how many you can spot. Look by the water, but don't forget to look in the trees, too.

Look back at the words in dark print. Say each word. What vowel sound do you hear in each one?

Spelling Practice

Two vowels that come together in a word can spell a long-vowel sound. In a word with a **vowel pair**, you can hear the sound of the vowel that comes first, as in toes and tie.

LIST WORDS

1. beat *beat*
2. roads *roads*
3. mean *mean*
4. lay *lay*
5. main *main*
6. lower *lower*
7. pie *pie*
8. tie *tie*
9. toes *toes*
10. read *read*

Grouping Vowel Pairs

Write each **list word** under the heading that shows its vowel sound.

long **a** sound

1. ______________ 2. ______________

long **e** sound

3. ______________ 4. ______________

5. ______________

long **i** sound

6. ______________ 7. ______________

long **o** sound

8. ______________ 9. ______________

10. ______________

Word Clues

Write the **list word** that matches each clue.

1. most important ______________________
2. to stir or whip ______________________
3. foot parts ______________________
4. chickens do this to eggs ______________________
5. you do this with shoe laces ______________________
6. a dessert ______________________

Scrambled Letters

Unscramble the letters to make **list words**.
Then use the number code to write the answer to the riddle.

1. daros

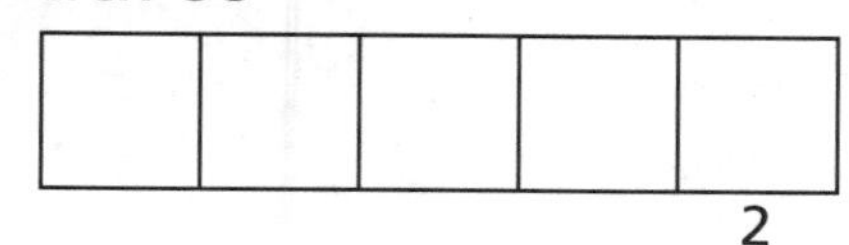

2. woler

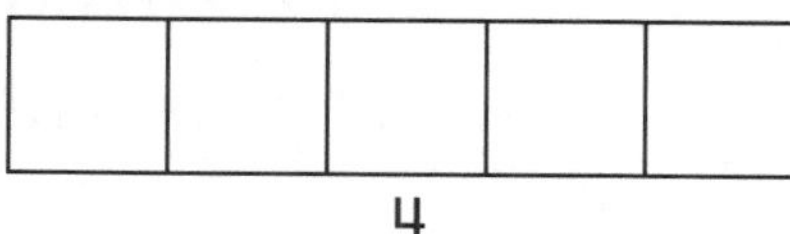

3. drea

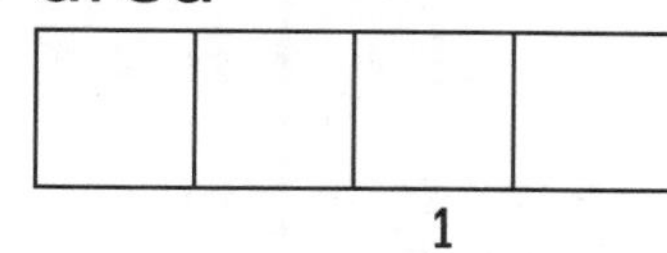

4. nema

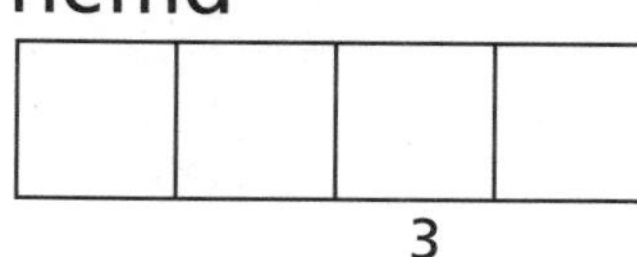

Write the letter with the number 1 under it on the first numbered line below. Do the same for numbers 2 through 4.

Riddle: What has a thousand teeth and no mouth?

Answer: ___   ___ ___ ___
1   2 3 4

Spelling and Writing

Proofreading

Each sentence has two mistakes. Use the proofreading marks to fix each mistake. Write the misspelled **list words** correctly on the lines.

Proofreading Marks

- ⬭ spelling mistake
- ⊙ add period
- ≡ capital letter

1. Frogs have webbed tose for swimming — 1. ______________
2. frogs ley their eggs in the water. — 2. ______________
3. A frog's mane diet is insects and worms — 3. ______________

Writing a Description

Write a description of a frog you've seen or would like to see. Proofread your description and fix any mistakes.

____

____

____

____

BONUS WORDS

- team
- faint
- toast
- bowl
- lie

Lessons 25–29 • Review

In Lessons 25–30, you learned how to spell words with the endings **ing**, **ed**, **s** or **es**, **er**, and **est**. You also learned the sound of vowels followed by **r** and the sound of vowel pairs.

Check Your Spelling Notebook

Look at the words in your spelling notebook. Which words for Lessons 25 through 29 did you have the most trouble with? Write them here.

____

____

Lesson 25

TIP **When r follows the vowels e, i, o, or u, it can make the ur sound, as in girl and word.**

List Words

first
turn
her
world

Write a **list word** that belongs in each group.

1. them, him,
2. Earth, planet,
3. third, second,
4. twirl, twist,

Lesson 26

TIP **The endings ing, ed, and s or es are added to base words to make new words, as in glasses. Add es to words that end in x, s, sh, or ch, as in boxes.**

List Words

- opening
- wants
- wishes
- worked

Write a **list word** that has the same base word as each word.

1. wishing ____________

2. wanted ____________

3. working ____________

4. opened ____________

Lesson 27

TIP **The final consonant in most short-vowel words is doubled when an ending is added: jog + ing = jogging.**

List Words

- gladdest
- running
- mixed
- sadder

Write a **list word** that means the same or almost the same as each word.

1. racing ____________

2. unhappier ____________

3. happiest ____________

4. blended ____________

Lesson 28

TIP **When a word ends in silent e, drop the e to add an ending that begins with a vowel, as in having. When a word ends in y after a consonant, change y to i to add the endings ed, es, er, and est, as in fried.**

List Words

baked
luckier
trades
serving

Write a **list word** to match each clue.

1. having more good things happening ____________
2. a helping of food ____________
3. cooked in an oven ____________
4. swaps ____________

Lesson 29

TIP **When a word has a vowel pair, the vowel you hear comes first, as in beat and roads.**

List Words

main
read
tie
toes

Write a **list word** that has the same vowel sound as each word.

1. rope ____________
2. kite ____________
3. game ____________
4. teeth ____________

Show What You Know

Lessons 25–29 Review

One word is misspelled in each set of **list words**. Fill in the circle next to the **list word** that is spelled incorrectly.

1.	○ wants	○ gurl	○ mixed	○ fried
2.	○ loves	○ sadder	○ boxes	○ roods
3.	○ wishs	○ sir	○ baked	○ pie
4.	○ lay	○ her	○ triming	○ sees
5.	○ word	○ bodys	○ beat	○ worked
6.	○ tie	○ first	○ wining	○ burning
7.	○ reached	○ having	○ turn	○ meen
8.	○ skurt	○ jogging	○ mean	○ were
9.	○ trades	○ gladest	○ sending	○ toes
10.	○ read	○ running	○ openning	○ world
11.	○ lower	○ glasses	○ worth	○ funnyest
12.	○ beat	○ skiping	○ luckier	○ worked
13.	○ carrys	○ hopped	○ turn	○ read
14.	○ serving	○ boxes	○ shoped	○ first
15.	○ baked	○ mixed	○ main	○ wurld
16.	○ her	○ toze	○ wants	○ burning
17.	○ haveing	○ word	○ lower	○ sending
18.	○ sees	○ her	○ beat	○ fryed
19.	○ pie	○ sending	○ glases	○ lay
20.	○ luves	○ were	○ reached	○ running

Spelling Words in Action

How does a starfish move?

Stars of the Sea

The starfish got its name because most starfish are shaped like stars.

Starfish live in the ocean. The bottom of each starfish arm is covered with tiny, tube-shaped feet. Each **foot** has a tiny suction pad on the end. The starfish uses these for crawling along the ocean floor.

Clams and oysters make a **good** meal for a starfish. The starfish wraps itself around the clam or oyster. **Soon** it pulls the shells apart. A starfish doesn't have a single **tooth**. It turns its **food** into a liquid and drinks it.

A starfish can do some amazing things. It can drop an arm if it is attacked. Then it grows a new one back. If a starfish is cut in two, each piece can grow into a new starfish. Now that's a pretty neat trick!

Look back at the words in dark print. Say each word. What vowel sound do you hear? What do you notice about the spelling for each word?

Spelling Practice

TIP

Two letters can stand for the $\overline{oo}$ sound, as in noon, or the oo sound, as in foot. Listen for the two sounds that are spelled **oo** in the **list words.**

LIST WORDS

1. foot *foot*
2. food *food*
3. soon *soon*
4. good *good*
5. hood *hood*
6. noon *noon*
7. room *room*
8. wood *wood*
9. boot *boot*
10. tooth *tooth*

Grouping Vowel Pairs

Write **list words** under the heading that shows the sound that **oo** stands for in each one.

oo as in moon

1. ____________ 2. ____________

3. ____________ 4. ____________

5. ____________ 6. ____________

oo as in book

7. ____________ 8. ____________

9. ____________ 10. ____________

Word Groups

Write the **list word** that belongs with each group.

1. arm, leg, ____________________
2. shoe, sneaker, ____________________
3. hat, cap, ____________________
4. great, OK, ____________________
5. morning, night, ____________________
6. fang, tusk, ____________________

Story

Write **list words** to finish the story.

"Dinner will be ready ____________________ ," said Rabbit. He set the table in the dining ____________________ . "I am really hungry," said Frog. "I haven't eaten since ____________________ ," said Squirrel.

As the ____________________ burned in the fireplace, Rabbit served the ____________________ to his friends.

Spelling and Writing

Proofreading

Proofreading Marks

- (oval) spelling mistake
- ⊙ add period
- (delete mark) take something out

The paragraph has six mistakes. Use the proofreading marks to fix each mistake. Write the misspelled **list words** correctly on the lines.

A shark's touth is very sharp They are are gud swimmers. Sharks will eat almost anything. Even an old boot could be fude for a a shark.

1. ______________
2. ______________
3. ______________

Writing a Narrative Paragraph

What is your favorite sea animal? Write a paragraph about it. Tell why you like it. Tell what it looks like.

____

____

____

____

BONUS WORDS

- brook
- pool
- wool
- cool
- loose

Spelling Words in Action

What color is Ms. Claypot's hair?

Ms. Claypot

Who is Ms. Claypot? She never makes any **noise**, not one little **sound**. She never wears a **frown**, but always has a big smile. She has green hair! Ms. Claypot is not a **toy**. She is a flower pot.

To make Ms. Claypot you will need: a clay pot, a dish, some **soil**, grass seeds, paper, glue, and scissors.

Turn the pot upside-down. Cut eyes, a nose, and a **mouth** out of paper. Glue them on the side of the pot to make her face. **Now** put the soil on top of her head. Scatter the seeds on top of the soil. Then put Ms. Claypot on a dish filled with water. Set her in a sunny place.

Always keep water in her dish. It will soak up through the clay pot and feed the seeds at the top. In a few weeks, Ms. Claypot will grow green "hair." Don't be surprised if she soon needs a haircut!

Look back at the words in dark print. Say each word. What words have the oi sound you hear in noise? Which words have the ou sound you hear in sound?

Spelling Practice

The sound **oi** can be spelled **oy** or **oi**, as in toy and oil. The sound **ou** can be spelled **ow** or **ou**, as in now and sound. Listen for the **oi** and **ou** sounds in the **list words**.

LIST WORDS

1. sound *sound*
2. frown *frown*
3. soil *soil*
4. mouth *mouth*
5. now *now*
6. toy *toy*
7. oil *oil*
8. spoil *spoil*
9. noise *noise*
10. owl *owl*

Spelling with oi and ou

Write each **list word** under the heading that shows the spelling of its **oi** or **ou** sound.

oi as in coin

1. ________________ 2. ________________

3. ________________ 4. ________________

ow as in how

5. ________________ 6. ________________

7. ________________

ou as in loud

8. ________________ 9. ________________

oy as in boy

10. ________________

Word Meaning

Write a **list word** to match each meaning.

1. a noise ______________________
2. something to play with ______________________
3. an opening in the face ______________________
4. a night bird that hoots ______________________
5. at this time ______________________
6. dirt ______________________

Word Puzzle

Write **list words** to fill in the puzzle. Then read down the shaded boxes to answer the riddle.

1. a sad look on someone's face
2. dirt
3. a liquid used for cooking
4. to ruin or break something
5. a bad or loud sound

Riddle: If I lose an eye, I'll still have a nose. What am I?

Answer: ______________________

Spelling and Writing

Proofreading

Proofreading Marks

- (oval) spelling mistake
- ⊙ add period
- ^ add something

The paragraph has six mistakes. Use the proofreading marks to fix each mistake. Write the misspelled **list words** correctly on the lines.

An owel lives in the woods It says, "Whoo, whoo" when it opens its mowth Can you make a noyse that sounds like an owl

1. ____________
2. ____________
3. ____________

Writing a Make-Believe Story

What if you found a magic bean like Jack in the Beanstalk? What if you planted a penny and grew a money tree? Write a make-believe story.

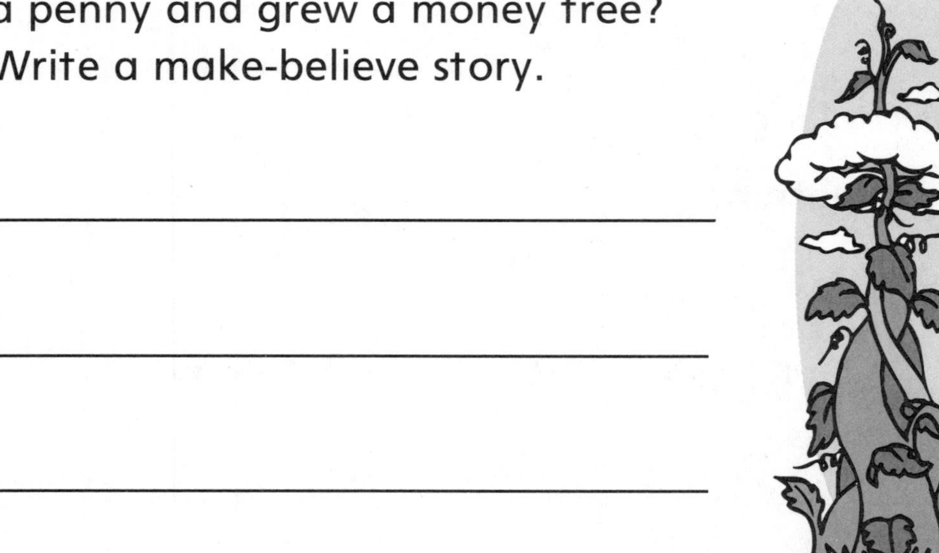

____

____

____

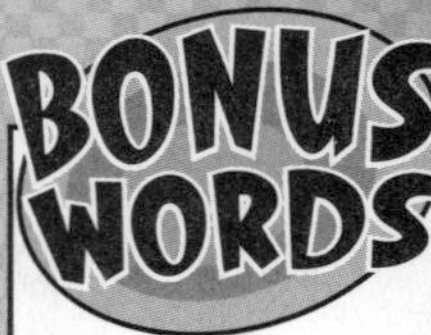

crowd

tower

around

pound

boil

Spelling Words in Action

What is the name of the camp in this story?

A Camp That's "A-OK!"

They **call** it the "U.S. Space Camp." There is one near Huntsville, Alabama. Children go there to learn about space.

The camp lasts a week. Children love it **because** there are many things to do. You can **talk** to people who know about space travel. You get to see some really **tall** rockets that once took people into space. You can help **draw** a plan for a spaceship. You do your drawing on a computer. Then build a rocket of your own. Watch it zoom into the sky.

There is more fun when you take a make-believe trip into space. It feels just like the real thing! Your trip might be to the moon. You'll learn what it's like to **walk** on the moon.

Look back at the words in dark print. Say each word. What vowel sound do you hear?

The ô sound can be spelled three different ways: **au**, as in because, **aw**, as in draw, and **a**, as in call.

LIST WORDS

1. call *call*
2. wall *wall*
3. draw *draw*
4. tall *tall*
5. ball *ball*
6. paw *paw*
7. crawl *crawl*
8. talk *talk*
9. because *because*
10. walk *walk*

Spelling Practice

Spelling with the ô Sound

Write each **list word** under the heading that spells its ô sound.

aw as in claw

1. ______________ 2. ______________

3. ______________

a as in all

4. ______________ 5. ______________

6. ______________ 7. ______________

8. ______________ 9. ______________

au as in haul

10. ______________

Word Meaning

Write the **list word** that means the same or almost the same as each word.

1. speak ____________ 2. high ____________

3. sketch ____________ 4. creep ____________

5. foot ____________ 6. yell ____________

Word Search

There are four **list words** in the puzzle. They may go across or down. Circle each word. Then, write the words on the lines.

W	A	L	L	E	M	S
H	X	P	B	S	U	T
B	E	C	A	U	S	E
A	R	E	L	P	R	N
L	W	A	L	K	C	A
E	C	L	M	J	Y	N

1. ____________

2. ____________

3. ____________

4. ____________

Spelling and Writing

Proofreading

The paragraph has six mistakes. Use the proofreading marks to fix each mistake. Write the misspelled **list words** correctly on the lines.

Proofreading Marks

spelling mistake
⊙ add period
≡ capital letter

Imagine getting a phone cawl from space maybe you'll tauk to a friend who lives on a space station. That's a long distance call becuz space is a lot of miles away

1. ________________

2. ________________

3. ________________

Writing Questions

What would you like to know about space travel? Write some questions you have about space travel. Proofread your questions and fix any mistakes.

____

____

BONUS WORDS

straw
hall
dawn
salt
automobile

Spelling Words in Action

What can you make with a plastic bottle?

Recycling Is for the Birds

Don't **untie** that garbage bag to throw away an empty plastic bottle! Recycle the bottle. **Remake** it into a birdfeeder.

First, wash out the bottle. Then, cut a large hole in the side. The hole should be about two inches from the bottom of the bottle.

Next, decorate the bottle with markers. Then, tie a string around the neck of the bottle. Replace the bottle cap if you have it.

Fill the bottom of the bottle with bird seed. Then, hang it from the branch of a tree.

Remember to check and **recheck** your birdfeeder. Make sure it always has some food in it. The birds will be **unhappy** if it is empty. It would be **unkind** not to keep it full.

Now sit back and enjoy watching the birds!

Look back at the words in dark print. Say each word. What do you notice about the beginning of each word?

Spelling Practice

TIP

A **prefix** is a word part that is added to the beginning of a base word. The prefix **un** means not or the opposite, as in unkind. The prefix **re** means back or do again, as in reread.

LIST WORDS

1. unkind *unkind*
2. unlike *unlike*
3. retold *retold*
4. reread *reread*
5. unhappy *unhappy*
6. recheck *recheck*
7. remake *remake*
8. return *return*
9. unlock *unlock*
10. untie *untie*

Spelling with Prefixes

Write each **list word** next to its number. Circle the prefix in each word.

1. ________________ 2. ________________

3. ________________ 4. ________________

5. ________________ 6. ________________

7. ________________ 8. ________________

9. ________________ 10. ________________

Word Addition

Write a **list word** to match each meaning.
Add a prefix to the underlined base word.

1. not <u>like</u> ____________
2. <u>make</u> again ____________
3. not <u>kind</u> ____________
4. not <u>happy</u> ____________
5. opposite of <u>lock</u> ____________
6. <u>told</u> again ____________
7. <u>read</u> again ____________
8. <u>check</u> again ____________

Scrambled Letters

Unscramble the letters to make **list words**.
Then, use the number code to answer the riddle.

1. cekchre

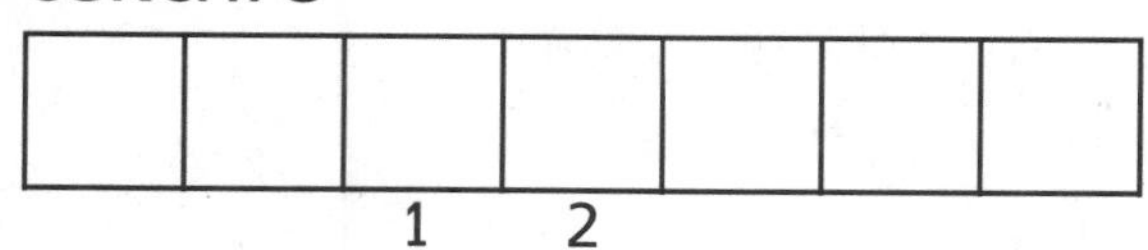

2. tineu

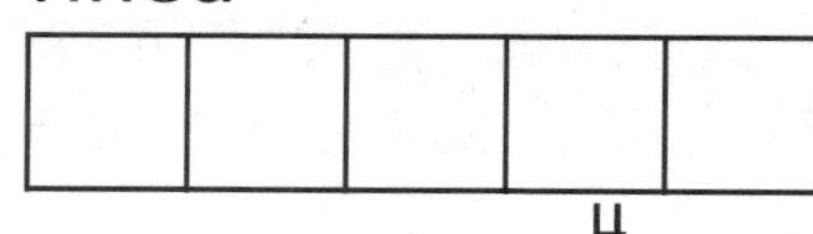

3. eadrer

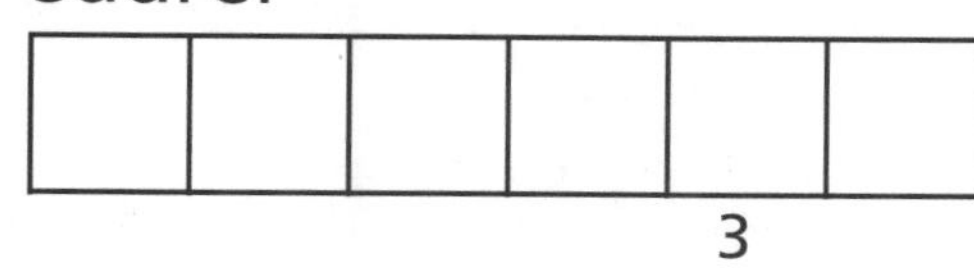

4. rurent

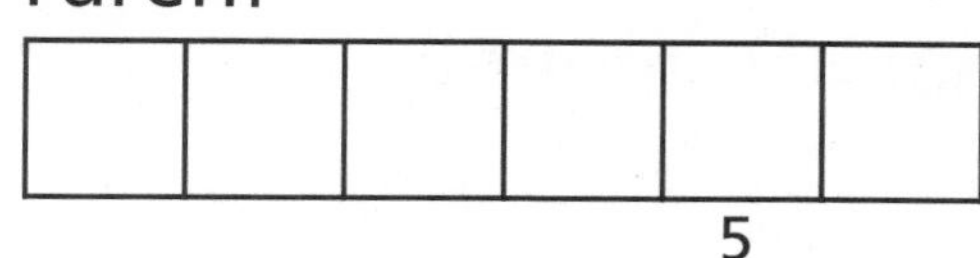

Find the letter with the number 1 under it. Write that letter on the line below that has the number 1 under it. Do the same for the numbers 2 through 5.

Riddle: What has four legs, a back, two arms, and no head?

Answer: a ___ ___ ___ ___ ___
1 2 3 4 5

Spelling and Writing

Proofreading

Proofreading Marks	
⬭	spelling mistake
⊙	add period
~~e~~	take out something

The paragraph has six mistakes. Use the proofreading marks to fix each mistake. Write the misspelled **list words** correctly on the lines.

You can never be be unhapie when you recycle things. It's so much fun to remaik something into something different What you make will be unlyke anything made by by someone else.

1. ____________________

2. ____________________

3. ____________________

Writing Directions

Do you know how to make something by recycling? Write directions telling how to make it.

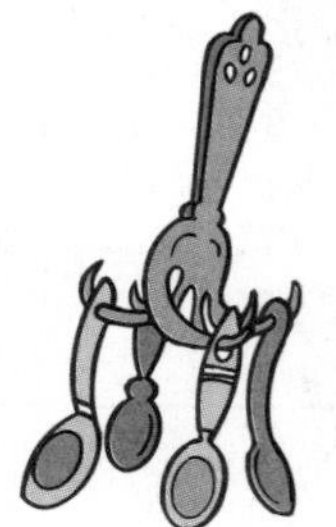

____

____

____

____

BONUS WORDS

rebuild
restart
redo
unhook
unsafe

Spelling Words in Action

What do you think a "hole in one" is?

Putt-Putt Golf

Some people call it miniature golf. It's called putt-putt golf, **too**. Whatever it's called, it's a lot of fun.

There's **no** secret to playing mini golf. If you **know** how to swing a golf club, you can play.

Putt-putt golf is like real golf, but the course is much smaller. You play with a real golf ball and golf club. You use the club to hit the ball. You try to get the ball into a **hole** called a cup. The idea is **to** get the ball into every hole with as few tries as possible.

Every golfer's dream is to get a "hole-in-**one**." This is when the ball goes into the cup on just one try. Wouldn't you like to say, "I played a **whole** game, got a hole in one, and **won**."

Look back at the words in dark print. Say each word. Which words have the same sound but different spellings?

Homonyms are words that sound alike but have different spellings and different meanings, such as **to, too,** and **two.**

Spelling Practice

LIST WORDS

1. hole *hole*
2. whole *whole*
3. no *no*
4. know *know*
5. not *not*
6. knot *knot*
7. ate *ate*
8. eight *eight*
9. to *to*
10. too *too*
11. two *two*
12. right *right*
13. write *write*
14. one *one*
15. won *won*

Spelling Homonyms

Match each **list word** with its clue. Write the word's number in the space.

1. an opening	___	2. complete	___
3. did eat	___	4. did not lose	___
5. to tie tightly	___	6. also	___
7. understand	___	8. in no way	___
9. not wrong	___	10. not yes	___
11. move toward	___	12. before two	___
13. a pair	___	14. four plus four	___
15. form letters	___		

Opposites

Write the **list word** that means the opposite or almost the opposite.

1. part ____________________
2. lost ____________________
3. untie ____________________
4. away ____________________
5. wrong ____________________
6. yes ____________________
7. uncertain ____________________
8. starved ____________________

Word Puzzle

Read each clue. Write **list words** to fill in the puzzle.

Across

1. one plus one
4. two minus one
5. one more than seven
7. an opening

Down

2. to form letters
3. in no way
6. also

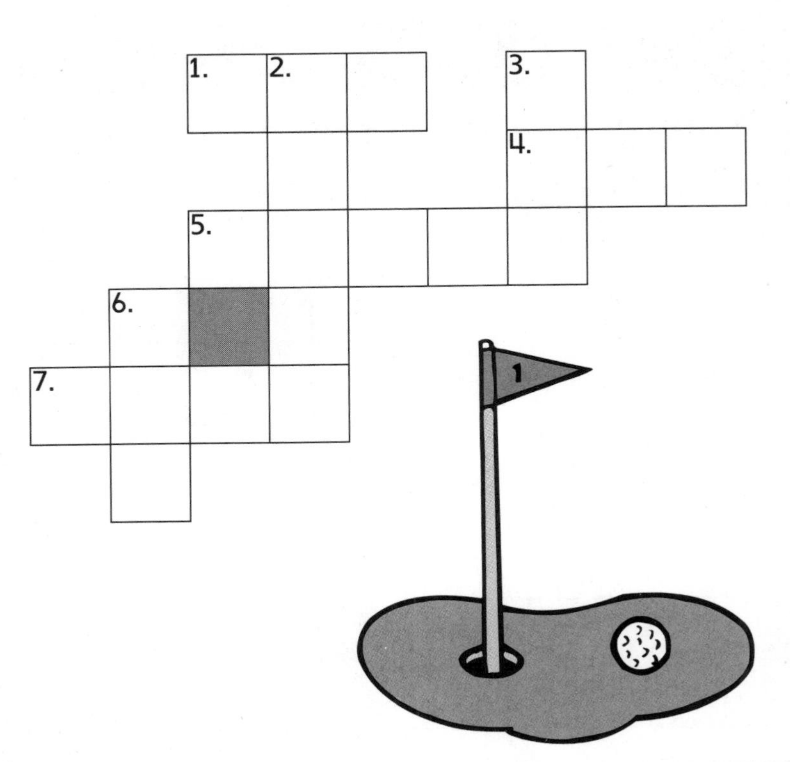

Spelling and Writing

Proofreading

The paragraph below has six mistakes. Use the proofreading marks to fix each mistake. Write the misspelled **list words** correctly on the lines.

Proofreading Marks

- (oval) spelling mistake
- (three lines) capital letter
- (loop) take something out

I put a a hole puzzle together by myself. I put all the write pieces together. I have too more puzzles to go. the next one has a thousand pieces. I'm not sure if i can do that one alone.

1. ______________

2. ______________

3. ______________

Writing a List

Many games use a ball. How many can you think of? Make a list of them.

____

____

____

____

BONUS WORDS

aunt
ant
for
four
deer
dear

Lessons 31–35 • Review

In Lessons 31–35 you learned how to spell words with the o͞o, **oo, ou, oi**, and **ô** sounds. You also learned about prefixes and homonyms.

Check Your Spelling Notebook

Look at the words in your spelling notebook. Which words for Lessons 31 through 35 did you have the most trouble with? Write them here.

____

____

Lesson 31

TIP **Words with oo can have two sounds. Listen to the oo sound, as in soon, and the oo sound, as in hood.**

List Words

- food
- good
- boot
- noon

Write the **list word** that belongs in each group.

1. morning, evening, ____________
2. eggs, bread, ____________
3. nice, kind, ____________
4. shoe, sneaker, ____________

Lesson 32

The letters oy or oi can spell the oi sound, as in toy and noise. The letters ow or ou can spell the ou sound, as in owl and sound.

List Words

mouth
now
soil
toy

Write the **list word** that matches each clue.

1. Play with this.

____

2. Plant seeds in this.

____

3. This is today.

____

4. Open this to talk.

____

Lesson 33

There are three spellings for the ô sound: au, as in because; aw, as in crawl; and a, as in ball.

List Words

paw
talk
tall
wall

Write the **list word** that belongs in each group.

1. foot, claw,

____

2. high, big,

____

3. floor, ceiling,

____

4. say, speak,

____

Lesson 34

TIP When you add a word part at the beginning of a base word, it's called a **prefix**. The prefix **un** means not or the opposite. The prefix **re** means back or do again.

List Words

recheck
unkind
unlike
return

Write the **list word** that means the same as the underlined words in each sentence.

1. That is not nice. ______________

2. Look over again. ______________

3. Let's go back. ______________

4. It's not the same as hers. ______________

Lesson 35

TIP You can hear the same sound in two words that have different meanings. These words are called **homonyms:** ate eight.

List Words

hole
whole
right
write

Write a **list word** to finish each sentence.

1. I will ______________ Jim a letter.

2. The worm crawled into the ______________.

3. He ate the ______________ pizza.

4. She has the ______________ answer.

Show What You Know

Lessons 31–35 Review

One word is misspelled in each set of **list words**. Fill in the circle next to the **list word** that is spelled incorrectly.

1.	○ fut	○ toy	○ call	○ untie
2.	○ unlike	○ paw	○ knowe	○ to
3.	○ owl	○ ate	○ good	○ spoyl
4.	○ tall	○ rechek	○ wood	○ no
5.	○ unloc	○ oil	○ boot	○ food
6.	○ not	○ too	○ craul	○ now
7.	○ soil	○ ball	○ noon	○ wholl
8.	○ return	○ becaus	○ wall	○ draw
9.	○ frawn	○ room	○ talk	○ two
10.	○ soon	○ one	○ hole	○ hod
11.	○ won	○ remake	○ wright	○ walk
12.	○ knot	○ unhappey	○ tooth	○ unkind
13.	○ call	○ boot	○ rereed	○ right
14.	○ noyse	○ tall	○ wood	○ hole
15.	○ good	○ not	○ untie	○ mauth
16.	○ one	○ sownd	○ unlike	○ room
17.	○ soon	○ right	○ tauk	○ owl
18.	○ won	○ return	○ draw	○ aight
19.	○ retolde	○ noon	○ paw	○ wall
20.	○ walk	○ ball	○ soyl	○ remake

Writing and Proofreading Guide

1. Choose something to write about.

2. Write your ideas. Don't worry about making mistakes.

3. Now proofread your work.
   Use these proofreading marks to check your work.

Proofreading Marks

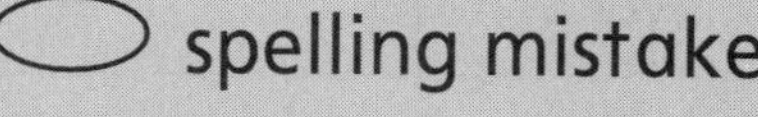

- spelling mistake
- capital letter
- add period
- add something
- add apostrophe
- take out something
- indent paragraph

the elephant has a a long trunke

4. Make your final copy.
   The elephant has a long trunk.

5. Share your writing.

Using Your Dictionary

The *Spelling Workout* Dictionary shows you many things about your spelling words.

The **entry word** listed in ABC order is the word you are looking up.

The **sound-spelling** or **respelling** tells how to say the word.

The **definition** tells what the word means.

hop (häp) to move by making short jumps [The bunny will hop into our garden.] **hops, hopped, hopping**

The **sample sentence** shows how to use the word.

Other **forms** of the word are listed.

Pronunciation Key

SYMBOL	KEY WORDS	SYMBOL	KEY WORDS	SYMBOL	KEY WORDS	SYMBOL	KEY WORDS
a	**a**sk, f**a**t	σο	l**oo**k, p**u**ll	b	**b**ed, du**b**	t	**t**op, ha**t**
ā	**a**pe, d**a**te	$\overline{σο}$	**oo**ze, t**oo**l	d	**d**id, ha**d**	v	**v**at, ha**v**e
ä	c**a**r, l**o**t	σu	**ou**t, cr**ow**d	f	**f**all, o**ff**	w	**w**ill, al**w**ays
				g	**g**et, do**g**	y	**y**et, **y**ard
e	**e**lf, t**e**n	u	**u**p, c**u**t	h	**h**e, a**h**ead	z	**z**ebra, ha**z**e
ē	**e**ven, m**ee**t	ʉ	f**u**r, f**e**rn	j	**j**oy, **j**ump		
				k	**k**ill, ba**k**e	ch	**ch**in, ar**ch**
i	**i**s, h**i**t	ə	**a** in **a**go	l	**l**et, ba**ll**	ŋ	ri**ng**, si**ng**er
ī	**i**ce, f**i**re		**e** in ag**e**nt	m	**m**et, tri**m**	sh	**sh**e, da**sh**
			e in fath**e**r	n	**n**ot, to**n**	th	**th**in, tru**th**
ō	**o**pen, g**o**		**i** in un**i**ty	p	**p**ut, ta**p**	*th*	**th**en, fa**th**er
ô	l**aw**, h**o**rn		**o** in c**o**llect	r	**r**ed, dea**r**	zh	**s** in plea**s**ure
σi	**oi**l, p**oi**nt		**u** in foc**u**s	s	**s**ell, pa**ss**		

able (ā bəl) can do something [He is able to tell jokes.]

afraid (ə frād) feeling scared [Jan is not afraid of anything.]

ago (ə gō) in the past [We met a year ago.]

alarm (ə lärm) the bell or buzzer on an alarm clock [I set my alarm for 6 a.m.] —**alarms**

all (ôl) **1** the whole thing [I can eat all my vegetables.] **2** every one [All my socks are blue.]

also (ôl so) too [Maria is my sister and also my friend.]

always (ôl wāz) every time [Lisa always does her homework.]

ant (ant) a small insect that lives in or on the ground [An ant crawled across the picnic table.] —**ants**

anything (en ē thiŋ) any object or event [There could be anything in that box!]

apple (ap əl) a red, green, or yellow fruit that is firm and juicy and grows on trees [Sam ate the red apple.] —**apples**

arch (ärch) **1** the curved part of something [There was an arch over the door.] **2** to curve or bend [My cat will often arch its back.] —**arches, arched, arching**

aren't (ärent) are not [I hope you aren't going to wear your new shoes in the mud!]

around (ə round) in a circle [The wheel turned around.]

ask (ask) **1** to use words to find out or get something [Let's ask Mom for a ride to the game.] **2** to invite [I will ask Jeff to my party.] —**asks, asked, asking**

ate (āt) did eat [Louisa ate her peas.]

a	ask, fat
ā	ape, date
ä	car, lot
e	elf, ten
ē	even, meet
i	is, hit
ī	ice, fire
ō	open, go
ô	law, horn
oi	oil, point
o͝o	look, pull
o͞o	ooze, tool
ou	out, crowd
u	up, cut
ʉ	fur, fern
ə	a in ago e in agent e in father i in unity o in collect u in focus
ch	chin, arch
ŋ	ring, singer
sh	she, dash
th	thin, truth
th	then, father
zh	s in pleasure

aunt (ant *or* änt) a sister of one's mother or father [My aunt is my father's little sister.] —**aunts**
automobile (ôt ə mə bēl) a car moved by an engine [Dad drives a red automobile.] —**automobiles**
away (ə wā) **1** to some other place [Billy moved away from here.] **2** in the proper place [Please put the rabbit away.] **3** not here [Our teacher is away this week.]

back (bak) **1** the part of the body on the other side of one's chest [The runner had a number on her back.] **2** the opposite of the front [Ellie sat in the back of the room.] **3** to move toward the rear [Can you back your bike into the garage?] **4** in the opposite direction [Seth ran there and back.] **5** in return [You do not have to pay back this money.] —**backs, backed, backing**
bad (bad) not pleasant [The bad weather kept everybody indoors.] —**worse, worst**
bait (bāt) food put on a hook or trap to catch fish or animals [She used a worm as bait when she fished.]
bake (bāk) to cook by dry heat [We will bake the bread for one hour.] —**bakes, baked, baking**
ball (bôl) anything with a round shape [Mo's ball of string rolled across the floor.] —**balls**
band (band) **1** a strip of some material used to wrap around or hold something together [The rubber band held the lid on the box.] **2** a group of musicians [The band played our favorite song.] —**bands**

beach (bēch) the sand or ground at the edge of an ocean or lake [Nate found pretty shells on the beach.] —**beaches**

beast (bēst) any large, four-footed animal [An elephant is a very large beast.] —**beasts**

beat (bēt) **1** to hit or strike again and again [I like to hear the rain beat against the roof.] **2** to win over [Our team will beat your team in basketball.] —**beats, beat, beaten, beating**

beaver (bē vər) an animal that can live on land and in water [The beaver built a dam across the stream.] —**beavers**

became (bē kām) did become [Gwen became ill after eating too much food.]

because (bē kôz) the reason for [I am happy today because it is my birthday.]

bed (bed) **1** a piece of furniture used for resting or sleeping [I changed the sheets on my bed.] **2** sleep [It is time for me to go to bed.] **3** a piece of ground where flowers grow [Dad planted tulips in the flower bed.] —**beds**

beg (beg) to ask for as charity or as a gift [I need to beg for a dollar from my mom.] —**begs, begged, begging**

behind (bē hīnd) **1** late or slow [We fell behind in our work.] **2** in back of [The man was sitting behind my seat.]

belt (belt) a strip of leather or cloth that goes around the waist [Rose wore a belt with her new dress.] —**belts**

bit (bit) a small piece or amount [He got a bit of dirt on his pants.] —**bits**

bite (bīt) to cut with the teeth [Don't bite off such a big piece.] —**bites, bit, biting**

a	ask, fat
ā	ape, date
ä	car, lot
e	elf, ten
ē	even, meet
i	is, hit
ī	ice, fire
ō	open, go
ô	law, horn
σi	oil, point
σ̆σ	look, pull
σ̄σ	ooze, tool
σu	out, crowd
u	up, cut
ʉ	fur, fern
ə	**a** in ago **e** in agent **e** in father **i** in unity **o** in collect **u** in focus
ch	**ch**in, ar**ch**
ŋ	ri**ng**, si**ng**er
sh	**sh**e, da**sh**
th	**th**in, tru**th**
th	**th**en, fa**th**er
zh	**s** in plea**s**ure

blanket (blaŋ kət) a warm covering used on a bed [A wool blanket will keep you warm at night.] —**blankets**

blow (blō) to force air out from the mouth [Blow out the candles.] —**blows, blew, blowing**

blue (blo͞o) having the color of the clear sky or the deep sea [My cat has blue eyes.] —**bluer, bluest**

blueberry (blo͞o ber ē) a small, round, dark blue berry that is eaten [Amy made a blueberry pie.] —**blueberries**

boat (bōt) a small vessel for traveling on water [We rode in a boat to the island.] —**boats**

body (bäd ē) the whole part of a person or animal [You should eat foods that are good for your body.] —**bodies**

boil (boil) to bubble up and become steam by being heated [Boil the water to make tea.] —**boils, boiled, boiling**

boot (bo͞ot) a covering of leather or rubber for the foot and part of the leg [My boot fell off my foot into the sticky mud.] —**boots**

born (bôrn) brought into life or being [Mario was born in July.]

bottle (bät l) a glass or plastic container for water, milk, or juice [The baby drank juice from a bottle.] —**bottles**

bowl (bōl) a deep, rounded dish [Susan ate a bowl of soup.] —**bowls**

box¹ (bäks) a cardboard or wooden container [The box had a lid.] —**boxes**

box² (bäks) to hit with the fist [Ed will box the champ tonight.] —**boxes, boxed, boxing**

a	**a**sk, f**a**t
ā	**a**pe, d**a**te
ä	c**a**r, l**o**t
e	**e**lf, t**e**n
ē	**e**ven, m**ee**t
i	**i**s, h**i**t
ī	**i**ce, f**i**re
ō	**o**pen, g**o**
ô	l**aw**, h**o**rn
oi	**oi**l, p**oi**nt
o͝o	l**oo**k, p**u**ll
o͞o	**oo**ze, t**oo**l
ou	**ou**t, cr**ow**d
u	**u**p, c**u**t
ʉ	f**u**r, f**e**rn
ə	**a** in ago **e** in agent **e** in father **i** in unity **o** in collect **u** in focus
ch	**ch**in, ar**ch**
ŋ	ri**ng**, si**ng**er
sh	**sh**e, da**sh**
th	**th**in, tru**th**
th	**th**en, fa**th**er
zh	**s** in plea**s**ure

boy (boi) a child who will grow up to be a man [The boy loved his father.] —**boys**

brave (brāv) full of courage [The brave firefighter saved the baby.] —**braver, bravest**

bread

bread (bred) a loaf baked from dough made of flour and other things [We sliced the bread to make wheat toast.] —**breads**

brook (broŏk) a small stream [Freddy jumped across the brook.] —**brooks**

bunny (bun ē) a rabbit [The bunny hopped away.] —**bunnies**

burn (burn) **1** to be on fire [The logs will burn for a few hours.] **2** to injure by heat [The hot stove will burn your hand.] **3** to feel hot [Your face will burn if you have a fever.] —**burns, burned, burning**

by (bī) near [The child is by her mother.]

call (kôl) **1** to shout or yell [I heard you call for your brother.] **2** to telephone [I need your phone number to call you.] —**calls, called, calling**

camera (kam ər ə *or* kam rə) a closed box for taking photographs [Judy took a photograph of her dog with a camera.] —**cameras**

canary (kə ner ē) a small, yellow songbird kept as a pet in a cage [The canary sang all morning.] —**canaries**

candle (kan dəl) a piece of wax with a wick that gives off light when burned [We lit a candle in the dark room.] —**candles**

can't (kant) cannot [Willie can't find his shoes.]

carry (ker ē) to take from one place to another [Jenny will carry Ben's books from school.] —**carries, carried, carrying**

cart (kärt) a small wagon [He put the lettuce in a grocery cart.] —**carts**

cent (sent) one penny [Maggie spent every cent she had on her sister's present.] —**cents**

cheese (chēz) a solid food made by pressing together curds of soured milk [Shirley made a ham and cheese sandwich.] —**cheeses**

cherry (cher ē) a small, round, sweet fruit [I like cherry ice cream the best.] —**cherries**

child (child) a young boy or girl [The child ran to her mother.] —**children**

circle (sur kel) **1** anything round [The children formed a circle around their teacher.] **2** to move around [The planets circle the sun.] —**circles, circled, circling**

city (sit ē) a very large town [Juan lives in a city with many tall buildings.] —**cities**

class (klas) one group or room of students in a school [Each class went on a field trip.] —**classes**

cherries

clean (klēn) **1** without dirt [The dishes were clean.] **2** to make neat and tidy [Please clean your desk.] —**cleaner, cleanest; cleans, cleaned, cleaning**

clue (klo͞o) a thing that helps to solve a puzzle [The clue helped the police find the robber.] —**clues**

coach (kōch) **1** a large, closed cart pulled by horses [The queen got out of the coach.] **2** a person who helps people play sports [My baseball coach said I played well.] **3** to help people play sports [Fred will coach the football team this year.] —**coaches, coached, coaching**

coat (kōt) something with sleeves that opens down the front and is worn over clothing to keep one warm or dry [Bonnie's new winter coat is made of wool.] —**coats**

coconut (kō kə nut) the large, round fruit of a coconut palm [I ate a coconut at the beach.] —**coconuts**

cold (kōld) very chilly [The weather was too cold for swimming.] —**colder, coldest**

color (kul ər) **1** the different shades of things, such as crayons or paints [Joan's favorite color is red.] —**colors 2** to use crayons or paints to fill in a picture [It is fun to color pictures with a friend.] —**colored, coloring**

cool (ko͞ol) not warm but not very cold [When the sun went down, the air became cool.] —**cooler, coolest**

corn (kôrn) a grain that grows in kernels on large cobs [Nell loves to eat corn on the cob.]

crash (krash) to fall, hit, or break with a very loud sound [Steve hoped that his sled would not crash into a tree.] —**crashes, crashed, crashing**

crater (krāt ər) a hollow that is shaped like a bowl [There is a crater at the mouth of the volcano.] —**craters**

crawl (krôl) to creep slowly on the ground [Alonzo's baby brother learned to crawl very early.] —**crawls, crawled, crawling**

crowd (kroud) a large group of people gathered together [A crowd filled the movie theater.] —**crowds**

crown (kroun) a headdress of gold and jewels worn by a king or queen [The queen's crown had diamonds and rubies in it.] —**crowns**

a	**a**sk, f**a**t
ā	**a**pe, d**a**te
ä	c**a**r, l**o**t
e	**e**lf, t**e**n
ē	**e**ven, m**ee**t
i	**i**s, h**i**t
ī	**i**ce, f**i**re
ō	**o**pen, g**o**
ô	l**aw**, h**o**rn
oi	**oi**l, p**oi**nt
o͝o	l**oo**k, p**u**ll
o͞o	**oo**ze, t**oo**l
ou	**ou**t, cr**ow**d
u	**u**p, c**u**t
ʉ	f**u**r, f**e**rn
ə	**a** in ago **e** in agent **e** in father **i** in unity **o** in collect **u** in focus
ch	**ch**in, ar**ch**
ŋ	ri**ng**, si**ng**er
sh	**sh**e, da**sh**
th	**th**in, tru**th**
th	**th**en, fa**th**er
zh	**s** in plea**s**ure

crown

cub (kub) babies of certain animals such as bears or lions [The mother bear kept her cub close to her.] —**cubs**

curtain (kurt n) a piece of cloth hung at a window or in front of a stage [When the curtain was raised, the play began.] —**curtains**

cut (kut) to make an opening in with a knife or other sharp tool [Mike cut his chin while he was shaving.] —**cuts, cut, cutting**

cute (kyo͞ot) pretty or pleasing [Everyone thought that the baby monkeys were cute.] —**cuter, cutest**

dawn (dôn) the beginning of day [The rooster crowed at dawn.] —**dawns**

dear (dir) **1** much loved [Reza is my dear friend.] **2** a polite form of address in a letter [He began the letter with "Dear Aunt Betty."] —**dearer, dearest**

deep (dēp) far down, far in, or far back [The water in the lake was very deep.] —**deeper, deepest**

deer (dir) a swift-running, hoofed animal [We saw a deer in the forest.] —**deer**

dirt (durt) matter that makes things unclean [Roy got dirt on his clean shirt.]

doesn't (duz ənt) does not [Marsha doesn't have a pet.]

draw (drô) to make a picture with pencils, pens, or crayons [Alice likes to draw horses.] —**draws, drew, drawn, drawing**

due (do͞o) owed or expected [My library book is due today.]

dust (dust) **1** fine, powdery material in the air [The dust from the dirt road made me cough.] **2** to wipe the dust from [Please dust the table.] —**dusts, dusted, dusting**

Ee

eagle (ē gəl) a large, strong bird [The eagle soared above the hills.] —**eagles**

ear (ir) either one of the two organs in the head through which sound is heard [The cute dog had one ear up and one ear down.] —**ears**

easy (ē zē) not hard to do [It was easy for Tom to learn to ride the bike.] —**easier, easiest**

eight (āt) the next number after seven [This cup holds eight ounces of water.]

enjoy (en joi) to get pleasure from [I enjoy reading books.] —**enjoys, enjoyed, enjoying**

face (fās) **1** the front of the head [Our teacher had a big smile on her face.] —**faces 2** to turn toward something [Please face the class.] —**faces, faced, facing**

faint (fānt) **1** weak [I heard a faint whisper.] **2** to fall into a sleep-like state [He will faint at the sight of blood.] —**faints, fainted, fainting**

far (fär) not near [My grandparents live far from our house.] —**farther, farthest**

farm (färm) a piece of land with buildings where crops and animals are raised [Tony's uncle has many cows on his farm.] —**farms**

feed (fēd) to give food to [Ryan will feed the fish.] —**feeds, fed, feeding**

fell (fel) dropped to a lower place [It hurt when I fell out of the tree.]

few (fyo͞o) not many [Yes, I'll have a few raisins.]

find (fīnd) to get something by looking for it [I hope I find my dime.] —**finds, found, finding**

fine[1] (fīn) **1** very good [You did a fine job on your homework!] **2** having very small parts [The beach has very fine sand.] —**finer, finest**

fine[2] (fīn) money paid for a mistake [Kiyo paid a fine for her late library books.] —**fines**

fire (fīr) **1** burning flames [We told stories by the fire.] **2** to shoot off something [He will fire the starting gun.] **3** to tell someone to leave a job [He had to fire the worker who was late every day.] —**fires, fired, firing**

first (fʉrst) the number-one thing [Paul was the first runner to cross the finish line.]

fit (fit) to be the right size [You need skates that fit your feet.] —**fits, fitted, fitting**

fix (fiks) to repair or mend [Can you fix the broken chair?] —**fixes, fixed, fixing**

flat (flat) smooth and level [The top of the table is flat.] —**flatter, flattest**

flew (flo͞o) moved through the air, usually with wings [The plane flew above the clouds.]

floor (flôr) the bottom part of a room on which one walks [We put a rug on the floor.] —**floors**

fog (fôg) a thick mist that is hard to see through [We couldn't see the road in the fog.]

fold (fōld) to bend something over upon itself so that one part is on top of another [Please fold the napkins.] —**folds, folded, folding**

food (fo͞od) a thing we eat to live and grow [We cooked the food in the oven.] —**foods**

a	**a**sk, f**a**t
ā	**a**pe, d**a**te
ä	c**a**r, l**o**t
e	**e**lf, t**e**n
ē	**e**ven, m**ee**t
i	**i**s, h**i**t
ī	**i**ce, f**i**re
ō	**o**pen, g**o**
ô	l**aw**, h**o**rn
oi	**oi**l, p**oi**nt
o͝o	l**oo**k, p**u**ll
o͞o	**oo**ze, t**oo**l
ou	**ou**t, cr**ow**d
u	**u**p, c**u**t
ʉ	f**u**r, f**e**rn
ə	**a** in ago **e** in agent **e** in father **i** in unity **o** in collect **u** in focus
ch	**ch**in, ar**ch**
ŋ	ri**ng**, si**ng**er
sh	**sh**e, da**sh**
th	**th**in, tru**th**
th	**th**en, fa**th**er
zh	**s** in plea**s**ure

foot (fo͝ot) **1** the part of the body on which people or animals stand [Mick rested his foot on the stool.] **2** a twelve-inch measure [The snow was more than a foot deep.] —**feet**

for (fôr) in order to be, keep, have, get, or read [He swims for exercise.]

forest (fôr əst) a thick growth of trees [Deer live in the forest.] —**forests**

four (fôr) the cardinal number between three and five [Two plus two equals four.]

fox (fäks) a wild animal of the dog family with reddish fur and a long, bushy tail [The red fox cared for her young ones.] —**foxes**

fresh (fresh) newly made, got, or grown [A fresh tomato tastes delicious.] —**fresher, freshest**

fried (frīd) cooked over heat in oil or fat [Herman loves fried eggs.]

friend (frend) someone a person knows well and likes [I like to play with my friend Sara.] —**friends**

frog (frôg) a small, croaking pond animal that jumps [The tadpole will grow up to be a frog.] —**frogs**

frog

from (frum) **1** starting at [Dad works from nine until five.] **2** out of [Take your book from the desk.] **3** made or sent by [Simon got a gift from his aunt.]

frown (fro͞un) a sad look on a person's face [Gina's frown became a smile when she saw the funny clown.] —**frowns**

fry (frī) to cook over heat in oil or fat [I will fry the egg in butter.] —**fries, fried, frying**

funny (fun ē) causes laughter [The clown's baggy pants looked funny.] —**funnier, funniest**

gate (gāt) a swinging door in a fence [Dean opened the gate to let me in.] —**gates**

gather (ga*th* ər) to bring or come together in one place or group [Gather your books.] —**gathers, gathered, gathering**

gentle (jent l) mild, soft, or easy [A gentle breeze cooled my face.] —**gentler, gentlest**

get (get) **1** to come to own [Mom said we could get a puppy.] **2** to arrive somewhere [We may get to Texas by noon.] **3** to go and bring [Please get me an apple.] —**gets, got, gotten, getting**

gift (gift) a present [I bought a gift for my mother.] —**gifts**

girl (gʉrl) a female child [Maria is the girl with the red bow in her hair.] —**girls**

glad (glad) happy [I am glad that you came to see me.] —**gladder, gladdest**

glass (glas) **1** a hard substance that breaks easily and lets light through [The window pane is made of glass.] **2** a lens people use to help them see [I will look through the glass to read the small print.] **3** a thing to drink out of that is often clear and does not have a handle [Pour milk into the glass.] —**glasses**

glove (gluv) a covering for the hands to keep them warm or protect them [Lance lost his golf glove.] —**gloves**

go (gō) to move from one place to another [Bea will go to your house at noon.] —**goes, went, gone, going**

goat (gōt) an animal like a sheep that has horns [The goat chews its cud.] —**goats**

good (go͝od) pleasing [The apples taste very good.] —**better, best**

a	**a**sk, f**a**t
ā	**a**pe, d**a**te
ä	c**a**r, l**o**t
e	**e**lf, t**e**n
ē	**e**ven, m**ee**t
i	**i**s, h**i**t
ī	**i**ce, f**i**re
ō	**o**pen, g**o**
ô	l**aw**, h**o**rn
oi	**oi**l, p**oi**nt
o͝o	l**oo**k, p**u**ll
o͞o	**oo**ze, t**oo**l
ou	**ou**t, cr**ow**d
u	**u**p, c**u**t
ʉ	f**u**r, f**e**rn
ə	**a** in ago **e** in agent **e** in father **i** in unity **o** in collect **u** in focus
ch	**ch**in, ar**ch**
ŋ	ri**ng**, si**ng**er
sh	**sh**e, da**sh**
th	**th**in, tru**th**
th	**th**en, fa**th**er
zh	**s** in plea**s**ure

grass (gras) green plants with narrow, pointed leaves that cover lawns and meadows [We mow the grass every week in the summer.]

gray (grā) a color between black and white [The sky was gray and full of dark clouds.]

greedy (grēd ē) wanting or taking all that one can get [The greedy boy ate all the cookies.] —**greedier, greediest**

grew (gro͞o) **1** became large or older [Nina grew four inches in one year.] **2** raised [The farmer grew beans last year.]

growl (groul) to make a low, rumbling, threatening sound in the throat [Dogs growl when they are angry.] —**growls, growled, growling**

gum[1] (gum) something sticky to chew [We do not chew gum in school.]

gum[2] (gum) the part of the mouth that holds the teeth [Melissa felt a new tooth in the baby's gum.] —**gums**

had (had) owned or held [The cat had a bell around its neck.]

half (haf) either of two equal parts of something [Five is half of ten.] —**halves**

hall (hôl) a passageway from which doors open into rooms [My room is at the end of the hall.] —**halls**

handle (han dəl) **1** the part by which something is lifted, held, or turned [Lana picked up the mug by the handle.] **2** to hold or touch [You must handle the kittens gently.] —**handles, handled, handling**

hard (härd) **1** not soft [Luke likes hard, crunchy crackers.] **2** not easy [It's hard to do outdoor work on a hot day.] —**harder, hardest**

have (hav) own or hold [I have a bowl of grapes.] —**has, had, having**

head (hed) **1** the part of the body above the neck [Diane wore a hat on her head.] **2** the front or top of something [Wait for me at the head of the line.] —**heads**

healthy (hel thē) well [Exercise to keep healthy.] —**healthier, healthiest**

heat (hēt) **1** great warmth [The heat made me sleepy.] **2** to make or become warm or hot [The fire will heat the room.] —**heats, heated, heating**

heavy (hev ē) weighing very much [That piano is very heavy.] —**heavier, heaviest**

heel (hēl) the back part of the foot [I have a blister on my heel.] —**heels**

help (help) to do something to make a thing easier for someone [I like to help Dad dry the dishes.] —**helps, helped, helping**

her (hʉr) having to do with a girl or a woman [Mom had a smile on her face.]

hide (hīd) to put or keep out of sight [I will hide the gift in my closet.] —**hides, hid, hidden, hiding**

hill (hil) ground that is a little higher than the land around it [We could see far from the top of the hill.] —**hills**

him (him) having to do with a boy or man [Ivan asked me to help him.]

his (hiz) belonging to him [His book is on the desk.]

a	**a**sk, f**a**t
ā	**a**pe, d**a**te
ä	c**a**r, l**o**t
e	**e**lf, t**e**n
ē	**e**ven, m**ee**t
i	**i**s, h**i**t
ī	**i**ce, f**i**re
ō	**o**pen, g**o**
ô	l**aw**, h**o**rn
oi	**oi**l, p**oi**nt
oo	l**oo**k, p**u**ll
o͞o	**oo**ze, t**oo**l
ou	**ou**t, cr**ow**d
u	**u**p, c**u**t
ʉ	f**u**r, f**e**rn
ə	**a** in ago **e** in agent **e** in father **i** in unity **o** in collect **u** in focus
ch	**ch**in, ar**ch**
ŋ	ri**ng**, si**ng**er
sh	**sh**e, da**sh**
th	**th**in, tru**th**
th	**th**en, fa**th**er
zh	**s** in plea**s**ure

hole (hōl) an opening in something [There is a <u>hole</u> in my sock.] —**holes**
holiday (häl ə dā) a day on which most people do not have to work [We have a <u>holiday</u> next Monday.] —**holidays**
hood (hood) **1** a covering for the head [Jerry had a blue coat with a <u>hood</u>.] **2** the lid that covers the engine of a car [Brenda lifted the <u>hood</u> of the car.] —**hoods**
hop (häp) to move by making short jumps [The bunny will <u>hop</u> into our garden.] —**hops, hopped, hopping**
hope (hōp) to wish for or want very much [We <u>hope</u> that we can use our sleds today.] —**hopes, hoped, hoping**
horse (hôrs) a large animal with four legs, hoofs, a long tail, and a mane [Sweet Pea was a fine racing <u>horse</u>.] —**horses**
hour (our) sixty minutes [Dinner will be ready in one <u>hour</u>.] —**hours**
hug (hug) to clasp in the arms and hold close [The baby likes to <u>hug</u> her teddy bear.] —**hugs, hugged, hugging**
huge (hyōōj) very large [The horse seemed <u>huge</u> to the little girl.]

I'd (īd) **1** I had **2** I would **3** I should [<u>I'd</u> like an apple.]
I'm (īm) I am [<u>I'm</u> tired.]
inch (inch) a unit used to measure things [A quarter is about one <u>inch</u> wide.] —**inches**
isn't (iz ənt) is not [Scooter <u>isn't</u> his real name.]
it's (its) **1** it is [<u>It's</u> time to go.] **2** it has [<u>It's</u> been a fun day.]

joey (jō ē) a young kangaroo [The mother kangaroo cared for her joey.] —**joeys**

jog (jäg) to run at a slow, even pace [Pat will jog in the park each day.] —**jogs, jogged, jogging**

joy (joi) a very happy feeling [You could see the joy on his face when he won.]

just (just) exactly [Angela was just on time for class.]

keep (kēp) **1** to hold or save [Alex will keep his report card.] **2** to write down a record of something [Do you keep a diary?] **3** to continue [Keep calling until you get an answer.] —**keeps, kept, keeping**

key (kē) **1** a small metal piece that opens a lock [Lara uses a key to start her car.] **2** one of the flat parts that is pressed down on a typewriter or a piano [That key on the piano is broken.] —**keys**

kick (kik) to hit with the foot [Brian can kick the ball far.] —**kicks, kicked, kicking**

kind[1] (kīnd) sort or variety [What kind of ice cream do you like?] —**kinds**

kind[2] (kīnd) friendly, generous [My aunt is a kind person.] —**kinder, kindest**

knew (no͞o) was sure of [Quan knew what time it was.]

knot (nät) a loop in a string or ribbon that is pulled tight [The shoelaces were tied in a knot.] —**knots**

know (nō) **1** be sure of [Did you know the answer?] **2** to hear, feel, or see something [Susie says that she does not know Lee.] —**knows, knew, known, knowing**

lake (lāk) a large body of water with land all around [There are many fish in the lake.] **—lakes**

lamb (lam) a young sheep [The wool of the little lamb was soft and white.] **—lambs**

lay (lā) **1** to put or place [Lay your books on the table.] **2** to give an egg, as a chicken does [A hen will lay an egg in the nest.] **—lays, laid, laying**

led (led) showed the way [The guide led them along the path.]

let (let) to allow [They let me help.] **—lets, let, letting**

let's (lets) let us [Let's hurry to get to the show on time.]

lettuce (let əs) a plant with crisp, green leaves that is often used in salads [Do you like lettuce and tomato sandwiches?]

lie[1] (lī) to stretch one's body in a flat position [Lie down on the bed.] **—lies, lay, lying**

lie[2] (lī) **1** something said that is not true [What he said was a lie.] **2** to say what is not true [Do not lie to me.] **—lies, lied, lying**

line (līn) **1** a cord, rope, or string [She will hang the sheets on the line to dry.] **2** a long, thin mark [Draw a line under the best answer.] **3** a straight row [We stood in line at the bank.] **—lines**

list (list) **1** a set of words or numbers set down in order [Mom made a list of items she needed.] **2** to make a list [Please list the names of your friends for me.] **—lists, listed, listing**

lobster (läb stər) a large shellfish with big claws [Many people like to eat lobster.] **—lobsters**

lamb

a	**a**sk, f**a**t
ā	**a**pe, d**a**te
ä	c**a**r, l**o**t
e	**e**lf, t**e**n
ē	**e**ven, m**ee**t
i	**i**s, h**i**t
ī	**i**ce, f**i**re
ō	**o**pen, g**o**
ô	l**aw**, h**o**rn
oi	**oi**l, p**oi**nt
o͝o	l**oo**k, p**u**ll
o͞o	**oo**ze, t**oo**l
ou	**ou**t, cr**ow**d
u	**u**p, c**u**t
ʉ	f**u**r, f**e**rn
ə	**a** in ago **e** in agent **e** in father **i** in unity **o** in collect **u** in focus
ch	**ch**in, ar**ch**
ŋ	ri**ng**, si**ng**er
sh	**sh**e, da**sh**
th	**th**in, tru**th**
th	**th**en, fa**th**er
zh	**s** in pleasure

lock (läk) to fasten a door or safe [Please lock the door.] —**locks, locked, locking**

look (lo͝ok) to turn one's eyes in order to see [Look at your book.] —**looks, looked, looking**

loose (lo͞os) not firmly fastened [My front tooth is loose.] —**looser, loosest**

love (luv) **1** to have a deep and tender feeling for [My mother and father love me.] **2** to like very much [Al and Rita love Swiss cheese.] —**loves, loved, loving**

low (lō) **1** not high or tall [The batter swung at the low pitch.] **2** below others or less than usual [The hat was for sale at a low price.] —**lower, lowest**

lucky (luk ē) having good things happen by chance [Jim was lucky to have found a dime.] —**luckier, luckiest**

mad (mad) angry [My mother is mad at me for being late.] —**madder, maddest**

main (mān) the most important [A baby's main food is milk.]

many (men ē) a large number of [Many people go to the bank on payday.]

maple (mā pəl) a shade tree grown for its hard wood or sap, which is used to make syrup [I love maple syrup.] —**maples**

march (märch) to walk with regular, steady steps as soldiers do [I am going to march in the parade.] —**marches, marched, marching**

mare (mer) a female horse [My horse is a brown mare.] —**mares**

mask (mask) something worn over the face [Donna wore a scary Halloween mask.] —**masks**

math (math) a subject dealing with numbers and symbols [We learned how to add in math class today.]

may (mā) **1** might [This may be the wrong road.] **2** to be allowed [Yes, you may go out to play.]

mean[1] (mēn) to be a sign of [What does this letter mean?] —**means, meant, meaning**

mean[2] (mēn) unkind or not nice [Never be mean to your sister.] —**meaner, meanest**

meet (mēt) **1** to see someone for the first time [It's been very nice to meet you!] **2** to plan to be at a place where someone else plans to be, too [Let's meet in the gym after school.] **3** to be joined [The two rivers meet ahead.] —**meets, met, meeting**

met (met) saw someone for the first time [I met my neighbor yesterday.]

midnight (mid nīt) twelve o'clock at night [A new day begins after midnight.]

mile (mīl) a distance of 5,280 feet or 1.609 kilometers [We live a mile away.] —**miles**

mind (mīnd) **1** the thinking part of a person [Jason has a good mind for math.] **2** to care about [Would you mind helping me?] —**minds, minded, minding**

minute (min it) any of the sixty equal parts of an hour [There are sixty seconds in one minute.] —**minutes**

a	ask, fat
ā	ape, date
ä	car, lot
e	elf, ten
ē	even, meet
i	is, hit
ī	ice, fire
ō	open, go
ô	law, horn
oi	oil, point
oo	look, pull
ōō	ooze, tool
ou	out, crowd
u	up, cut
ʉ	fur, fern
ə	**a** in ago **e** in agent **e** in father **i** in unity **o** in collect **u** in focus
ch	**ch**in, ar**ch**
ŋ	ri**ng**, si**ng**er
sh	**sh**e, da**sh**
th	**th**in, tru**th**
th	**th**en, fa**th**er
zh	**s** in plea**s**ure

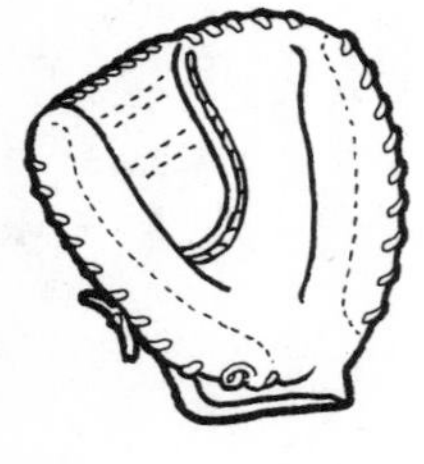
mitt

mitt (mit) a padded glove worn by baseball players [Sheila brought her catcher's mitt.] —**mitts**

mix (miks) to stir together [You can mix the flour and eggs.] —**mixes, mixed, mixing**

Monday (mun dā) the second day of the week [School begins on Monday.] —**Mondays**

month (munth) about a thirty-day period [Summer vacation begins in the month of June.] —**months**

moon (mo͞on) the largest heavenly body that can be seen in the night sky [A full moon can be quite bright.] —**moons**

more (môr) greater or larger [May I have more bread, please?]

most (mōst) almost all [Most children like to visit the zoo.]

mouth (mouth) the opening in the head used for eating and talking [She chews with her mouth closed.] —**mouths**

much (much) a large amount [We liked the movie very much.]

mule (myo͞ol) an animal that is a cross between a horse and a donkey [A mule can be a great help to a farmer.] —**mules**

must (must) has to [This hat must be Meg's.]

mustn't (mus ənt) must not [You musn't talk to strangers.]

Nn

nap (nap) **1** to sleep for a short time [Do you nap in the afternoon?] **2** a short sleep [The baby takes a nap twice a day.] —**naps, napped, napping**

neck (nek) the part of a person or animal that joins the head to the body [The man wore a tie around his neck.] —**necks**

new (no͞o) here for the first time [Pete's mom bought a new car.] —**newer, newest**

nibble (nib əl) to eat with quick, small bites [Mice like to nibble cheese.] —**nibbles, nibbled, nibbling**

nice (nīs) good, pleasant, or polite [Miss Lee is a nice teacher.] —**nicer, nicest**

no (nō) not so; opposite of yes [No, I did not call you.]

noise (noiz) a sound [The car's horn made a loud noise.] —**noises**

noon (no͞on) twelve o'clock in the daytime [We eat lunch at noon.]

nose (nōz) the part of the face that has two openings for breathing and smelling [Breathe through your nose, not your mouth.] —**noses**

not (nät) in no way [Let's not forget our manners.]

nothing (nuth iŋ) not a thing; zero [There was nothing left on the dish.]

now (nou) at this time [Please come over now for lunch.]

oak (ōk) the tree on which acorns grow and that is used for lumber [Aunt Lil sat down under the oak tree.] —**oaks**

ocean (ō shən) a large body of salt water that covers much of the Earth [Whales live in the ocean.] —**oceans**

oil (oil) **1** a greasy liquid used for cooking [Gary likes oil on his salad.] **2** a greasy liquid used for fuel [Some people use oil in lamps.] —**oils**

old (ōld) having been around for a long time [These are my old tennis shoes.]

one (wun) the number before two [You may take only one cookie.]

only (ōn lē) without any others [My friends were the only ones who knew the secret.]

opening (ō pən iŋ) **1** the act of making open [He is opening the door for us.] **2** an open place or hole [We fixed the opening in the wall with plaster.] —**openings**

orbit (ôr bit) the path of a heavenly body or satellite around another [The Earth will make an orbit around the Sun once every 365 days.] —**orbits**

oven (uv ən) an enclosed space for baking or roasting food [Mom put a turkey in the oven.] —**ovens**

over (ō vər) **1** above [The sky over us is blue.] **2** so that the other side is up [Flip the pancake over.] **3** again [Would you please read that story over?] **4** finished [At last, the trip was over.]

owl (oul) a bird with a large head, large eyes, a hooked beak, and sharp claws [The owl sleeps during the day.] —**owls**

own (ōn) **1** belonging to or having to do with oneself [I have my own toy.] **2** to have for oneself [We own two cars.] —**owns, owned, owning**

oyster (ois tər) a shellfish with a soft body that lives inside two rough shells joined together [A pearl grows inside an oyster.] —**oysters**

a	**a**sk, f**a**t
ā	**a**pe, d**a**te
ä	c**a**r, l**o**t
e	**e**lf, t**e**n
ē	**e**ven, m**ee**t
i	**i**s, h**i**t
ī	**i**ce, f**i**re
ō	**o**pen, g**o**
ô	l**aw**, h**o**rn
oi	**oi**l, p**oi**nt
o͝o	l**oo**k, p**u**ll
o͞o	**oo**ze, t**oo**l
ou	**ou**t, cr**ow**d
u	**u**p, c**u**t
ʉ	f**u**r, f**e**rn
ə	**a** in ago
	e in agent
	e in father
	i in unity
	o in collect
	u in focus
ch	**ch**in, ar**ch**
ŋ	ri**ng**, si**ng**er
sh	**sh**e, da**sh**
th	**th**in, tru**th**
th	**th**en, fa**th**er
zh	**s** in plea**s**ure

pack (pak) to put things together in something for carrying or storing [I will pack my suitcase tonight.] —**packs, packed, packing**

pad (pad) a number of sheets of paper fastened together along one edge [She wrote a story on a pad.] —**pads**

paint (pānt) **1** liquid color put on with a brush [The fresh paint gave the room a new look.] **2** to put color on with a brush [The boys began to paint the fence.] —**paints, painted, painting**

pale (pāl) having little color in the face or skin [He was very pale after his illness.] —**paler, palest**

park (pärk) **1** a place to rest or play [We flew kites in the park.] **2** to leave a car or truck in one place for a time [Did you park in the driveway?]

part (pärt) **1** a piece of something [Here's a part of my apple.] **2** a role in a play [Who will play the king's part?] **3** the line where one's hair is combed two ways [The part in Ted's hair is straight.] **4** to go away from each other [The twins wanted to stay together and never part.] —**parts, parted, parting**

paw (pô) the foot of an animal that has claws [The dog lifted its front paw.] —**paws**

peach (pēch) a pinkish-yellow fruit with fuzzy skin and a rough pit [I love to eat peach pie with ice cream.] —**peaches**

penny (pen ē) a coin worth one cent [Cora put the shiny new penny in her bank.] —**pennies**

people (pē pəl) persons [The streets were full of people.]

pet (pet) **1** an animal that is tamed and kept as a companion [That dog is our pet.] **—pets 2** to stroke or pat gently [I want to pet the horse.] **—pets, petted, petting**

piano (pē an ō) a large instrument with many wire strings in a case with a keyboard [Small hammers hit the piano strings when you press the keys.] **—pianos**

piano

a	**a**sk, f**a**t
ā	**a**pe, d**a**te
ä	c**a**r, l**o**t
e	**e**lf, t**e**n
ē	**e**ven, m**ee**t
i	**i**s, h**i**t
ī	**i**ce, f**i**re
ō	**o**pen, g**o**
ô	l**aw**, h**o**rn
ơi	**oi**l, p**oi**nt
ŏŏ	l**oo**k, p**u**ll
ōō	**oo**ze, t**oo**l
ou	**ou**t, cr**ow**d
u	**u**p, c**u**t
ʉ	f**u**r, f**e**rn
ə	**a** in ago **e** in agent **e** in father **i** in unity **o** in collect **u** in focus
ch	**ch**in, ar**ch**
ŋ	ri**ng**, si**ng**er
sh	**sh**e, da**sh**
th	**th**in, tru**th**
th	**th**en, fa**th**er
zh	**s** in plea**s**ure

pie (pī) a dish with filling in a crust [The pumpkin pie was still warm.] **—pies**

pillow (pil ō) a bag filled with feathers or foam used to rest the head on [I like to sleep on a soft pillow.] **—pillows**

pine (pīn) an evergreen tree with needles for leaves [It is fun to collect pine cones.] **—pines**

pint (pīnt) a measure of volume equal to one-half quart [I drank a pint of milk at lunch.] **—pints**

pipe (pīp) a long tube through which water, gas, or oil can flow [The water spilled out of the pipe.] **—pipes**

plan (plan) a way of doing something that has been thought out ahead of time [Dad has a plan for our summer vacation.] **—plans**

plane (plān) a short form of **airplane** [We took a plane to New York.] **—planes**

plate (plāt) a flat dish for food [Raul ate all the food on his plate.] **—plates**

play (plā) **1** to have fun [It is fun to play games.] **2** to make music [Helen is learning to play the flute.] **—plays, played, playing 3** a story acted out on a stage [Amal had a small part in the play at school.] **—plays**

plus (plus) added to [Two plus two equals four.] —**pluses**

pocket (päk ət) a small pouch sewed into clothing for carrying things [Diane kept a comb in her pocket.] —**pockets**

pond (pänd) a small lake [A frog jumped into the pond.] —**ponds**

pool (po͞ol) a small pond [Many frogs live in that pool.] —**pools**

pot

porcupine (pôr kyo͝o pīn) a wild animal having long, sharp spines [The spines of a porcupine are called quills.] —**porcupines**

pot (pät) a round pan for cooking [Gus cooked a whole pot of soup.] —**pots**

pound (pound) a unit of weight [I bought a pound of potatoes.] —**pounds**

pup (pup) a young dog [The little pup chewed on my slipper.] —**pups**

pup

purple (pʉr pəl) a color that is a mixture of red and blue [The king has a purple robe.]

push (po͞osh) to press against so as to move [I like to push my little sister on the swing.] —**pushes, pushed, pushing**

put (po͝ot) to set in a place [Please put your shoes away.] —**puts, put, putting**

quick (kwik) fast [We had time for a quick snack.] —**quicker, quickest**

quilt (kwilt) a bed covering made of layers of cloth and filling that are stitched together to form patterns [The top layer of the quilt was made of carefully sewn pieces.] —**quilts**

Rr

raccoon (ra ko͞on) a furry animal with black rings on its tail and a black mask over its eyes [The raccoon is active at night.] —**raccoons**

race (rās) **1** a contest of speed [Tanya won the race.] —**races 2** to go very fast [I will race you to the corner.] —**races, raced, racing**

rack (rak) a framework or stand for holding or displaying things [Choose a magazine from the rack.] —**racks**

rake (rāk) **1** a tool with a long handle that has a set of teeth at one end [A rake can be used to smooth the soil.] —**rakes 2** to gather or smooth with a rake [We will rake the leaves into a pile.] —**rakes, raked, raking**

reach (rēch) **1** to stretch out one's arm [Bess could not reach the top shelf.] **2** to arrive somewhere [The train will reach New York in one hour.] —**reaches, reached, reaching**

read[1] (rēd) to get the meaning of words that are written [Most people learn to read in first grade.] —**reads, read, reading**

read[2] (red) got the meaning of words that were written [Walt liked the book so much that he read it twice!]

real (rēl) true or not fake [Are those real pearls?]

rebuild (rē bild) to build again [They will rebuild the old house.] —**rebuilds, rebuilt, rebuilding**

recheck (rē chek) look again to see if something is all right [I must recheck my homework.] —**rechecks, rechecked, rechecking**

redo (rē do͞o) to do again or do over [I like to redo my favorite puzzle.] —**redoes, redid, redoing**

remake (rē māk) to make again [Tish will remake this old fur coat into a new jacket.] —**remakes, remade, remaking**

reread (rē rēd) to read again [Mark will reread his favorite book.] —**rereads, reread, rereading**

restart (rē stärt) to start again [Mom had to restart the motor.] —**restarts, restarted, restarting**

retold (rē tōld) said again [Grandpa retold the story to each of his seven grandchildren.]

return (ri turn) **1** to go or come back [When will you return from your trip?] **2** to bring or put back [Do not forget to return your library book.] —**returns, returned, returning**

right (rīt) **1** correct; not wrong [Greg was right about the weather.] **2** the hand or side that is not the left [Give me your right hand.]

river (riv ər) a large stream of water that flows into an ocean, lake, or other river [A long bridge was built over the river.] —**rivers**

road (rōd) a way for cars and trucks to go from one place to another [The road was very bumpy.] —**roads**

room (ro͞om) **1** a space in a building set off by walls [Every room in the house had a large window.] **2** enough space [Does your desk have enough room for another book?] —**rooms**

road

a	**a**sk, f**a**t
ā	**a**pe, d**a**te
ä	c**a**r, l**o**t
e	**e**lf, t**e**n
ē	**e**ven, m**ee**t
i	**i**s, h**i**t
ī	**i**ce, f**i**re
ō	**o**pen, g**o**
ô	l**aw**, h**o**rn
oi	**oi**l, p**oi**nt
o͝o	l**oo**k, p**u**ll
o͞o	**oo**ze, t**oo**l
ou	**ou**t, cr**ow**d
u	**u**p, c**u**t
ʉ	f**u**r, f**e**rn
ə	**a** in ago **e** in agent **e** in father **i** in unity **o** in collect **u** in focus
ch	**ch**in, ar**ch**
ŋ	ri**ng**, si**ng**er
sh	**sh**e, da**sh**
th	**th**in, tru**th**
th	**th**en, fa**th**er
zh	**s** in plea**s**ure

rule (rōōl) **1** a law [We have a rule at our house about no jumping on beds!] **2** to have power over [A new king was chosen to rule over the country.] —**rules, ruled, ruling**

run (run) to go by moving the legs very fast [Ashley will have to run to catch the bus.] —**runs, ran, run, running**

rush (rush) to move with great speed [Fatima had to rush to swim practice.] —**rushes, rushed, rushing**

sad (sad) unhappy [The sad children missed their old house.] —**sadder, saddest**

said (sed) used words to tell something [We all heard what Nancy said.]

sail (sāl) **1** a big sheet of canvas or cloth used on a boat or ship to catch the wind to make it move [We raised the sail on the boat.] —**sails** **2** to travel in a boat or ship [They planned to sail around the world.] —**sails, sailed, sailing**

salt (sôlt) a white substance used to flavor and preserve foods [Add a little salt to the soup.] —**salts**

same (sām) just like another; alike [Your bike is the same as mine.]

sandwich (san dwich) two or more slices of bread with a filling between them [I'd like a cheese sandwich.] —**sandwiches**

sat (sat) rested on one's bottom by bending at the waist [The lady sat on the park bench all day.]

satisfy (sat is fī) to meet the needs or wishes of; to make content; to please [Only first prize will satisfy him.] —**satisfies, satisfied, satisfying**

Saturn (sat ərn) the sixth planet away from the Sun [Saturn is known for its many rings.]

save (sāv) **1** to keep until later [Some people save their money in a bank.] **2** to keep someone or something from harm [The doctor tries to save lives.] —**saves, saved, saving**

saw[1] (sô) **1** a tool used to cut wood [Frank used a saw to cut the logs.] —**saws 2** to cut wood with this tool [Can you help me saw these boards?] —**saws, sawed, sawing**

saw[2] (sô) did see [I saw Bob yesterday.]

say (sā) to use words to tell something [Did you say your name was Margo?] —**says, said, saying**

scarlet (skär lət) very bright red [Mike's face turned scarlet from his sunburn.]

sea (sē) an ocean [Dave dreamed of sailing on the sea.] —**seas**

second (sek ənd) a part of a minute; an instant [Please, wait just a second.] —**seconds**

see (sē) **1** to look at [You can see the tall building from here.] **2** to understand [Now I see what you mean.] **3** to go to someone for help [When will you see a doctor about that foot?] —**sees, saw, seen, seeing**

seed (sēd) the part of a flowering plant that will grow into a new plant [The bean seed needs soil and water to grow.] —**seeds**

sell (sel) to give in return for money [Will you sell me this book for one dollar?] —**sells, sold, selling**

send (send) **1** to cause to go [I will send you home for lunch.] **2** to mail [She will send a letter to you soon.] —**sends, sent, sending**

a	ask, fat
ā	ape, date
ä	car, lot
e	elf, ten
ē	even, meet
i	is, hit
ī	ice, fire
ō	open, go
ô	law, horn
oi	oil, point
oo	look, pull
ōō	ooze, tool
ou	out, crowd
u	up, cut
ʉ	fur, fern
ə	a in ago e in agent e in father i in unity o in collect u in focus
ch	chin, arch
ŋ	ring, singer
sh	she, dash
th	thin, truth
th	then, father
zh	s in pleasure

serve (sûrv) **1** to do work for someone [Mona will serve as their maid.] **2** to offer food or drink [Mother will serve us a hot meal.] —**serves, served, serving**

set (set) **1** to put [You may set the plant over here.] **2** to make or become firm [Is the pudding set yet?] **3** to fix a date, time, or place [Julie set the date for her party.] **4** to sink [The Sun will set in the west.] —**sets, set, setting 5** a group of things [Max has a brand-new set of drums.] —**sets**

shape (shāp) the outer form [The cloud had the shape of a lamb.] —**shapes**

sheep (shēp) an animal related to the goat whose body is covered with heavy wool [I pet a sheep in the zoo.] —**sheep**

shell (shel) a hard outer covering [The turtle peeped out of its shell.] —**shells**

ship (ship) any vessel, larger than a boat, for traveling on deep water [They traveled by ship to Europe.] —**ships**

shirt (shûrt) a garment worn on the upper part of the body, usually having a collar and a buttoned opening [Peter wore a plaid shirt.] —**shirts**

shop (shäp) to go to a store to buy something [Toya likes to shop in the fabric store.] —**shops, shopped, shopping**

shore (shôr) land at the edge of a sea or lake [The boat was pulled up on the shore of the lake.] —**shores**

shot (shät) **1** the act or sound of shooting a gun [I heard the shot.] **2** a throw [José took a shot at the basket.] **3** the forcing of fluid into a person's body with a needle [The doctor gave me a shot.] —**shots**

shout (shout) **1** a loud call [We could hear Ted's shout for more nails.] **2** to call loudly [I had to shout because I was so far away.] —**shouts, shouted**

shrimp (shrimp) a small shellfish with a long tail used for food [We peeled the shrimp before we boiled it.] —**shrimp**

shut (shut) **1** to close [Please shut the windows if it rains.] —**shuts, shut, shutting 2** closed [Make sure the door is shut.]

shy (shī) timid [The puppy was too shy to play.] —**shyer, shyest**

sight (sīt) **1** something that is seen [The Grand Canyon is a pretty sight.] **2** the sense of seeing with one's eye [Jeff lost the sight in one eye.] —**sights**

silver (sil vər) **1** a white precious metal [She wore a silver necklace.] **2** a grayish-white color [Their car had silver trim.]

sir (sʉr) a polite way to speak to a man [No, sir, I did not see your dog.] —**sirs**

siren (sī rən) a thing that makes a loud, warning sound [The firefighter turned on the siren.] —**sirens**

skate (skāt) **1** to move along on ice [We like to skate in the winter.] —**skates, skated, skating 2** a shoe with a blade fastened on it for gliding on ice or rollers fastened for gliding on floors [Ben left the rink to lace his skate.] —**skates**

skin (skin) **1** the covering of the body of a person or animal [Franz scraped his skin when he fell.] **2** the outer covering of some fruits or vegetables [I peeled off the skin of the orange.] —**skins**

a	**a**sk, f**a**t
ā	**a**pe, d**a**te
ä	c**a**r, l**o**t
e	**e**lf, t**e**n
ē	**e**ven, m**ee**t
i	**i**s, h**i**t
ī	**i**ce, f**i**re
ō	**o**pen, g**o**
ô	l**aw**, h**o**rn
oi	**oi**l, p**oi**nt
oo	l**oo**k, p**u**ll
o͞o	**oo**ze, t**oo**l
ou	**ou**t, cr**ow**d
u	**u**p, c**u**t
ʉ	f**u**r, f**e**rn
ə	**a** in ago **e** in agent **e** in father **i** in unity **o** in collect **u** in focus
ch	**ch**in, ar**ch**
ŋ	ri**ng**, si**ng**er
sh	**sh**e, da**sh**
th	**th**in, tru**th**
th	**th**en, fa**th**er
zh	**s** in plea**s**ure

socks

skip (skip) **1** to move by hopping on one foot and then the other [Lucy will skip down the path.] **2** to pass over something [Since it is late, we will skip a few stories.] **—skips, skipped, skipping**

skirt (skʉrt) a piece of clothing that hangs from the waist of a woman or girl [Paula's skirt is made of wool.] **—skirts**

sleep (slēp) to be in the condition of rest with the eyes closed [Sometimes I dream when I sleep.] **—sleeps, slept, sleeping**

sleepy (slē pē) ready to fall asleep [Do you get sleepy at night?] **—sleepier, sleepiest**

slice (slīs) **1** a thin, broad piece of something [I will eat one slice of pizza.] **—slices 2** to cut [Tina will slice the melon for us.] **—slices, sliced, slicing**

smell (sməl) **1** to breathe in the odor of something [I smell fresh bread.] **—smells, smelled, smelling 2** an odor [That flower has a wonderful smell!]

smoke (smōk) the cloud that rises from something burning [We saw the smoke from their campfire.]

snake (snāk) a long, thin reptile with no legs [A snake will eat unwanted insects in your garden.] **—snakes**

so (sō) to such a degree or amount [Why are you so late?]

sock (säk) a warm covering for the foot that is worn inside a shoe [This sock does not match the other one.] **—socks**

soft (sôft) not hard [A baby's skin is soft.] **—softer, softest**

soil (soil) 1 the top layer of the Earth [This soil is good for plants.] **2** to make dirty [Please do not soil your new tennis shoes.] **—soils, soiled, soiling**

sold (sōld) gave something in return for money [Carl sold two baseball cards for ten dollars.]

soon (so͞on) in a short time [Soon it will be time for the flowers to bloom.] —**sooner, soonest**

sound (sound) a noise [The sound of the train was loud.] —**sounds**

space (spās) the area that stretches in all directions, has no limits, and contains all things in the universe [The Earth, the Sun, and all the stars exist in space.]

sparkle (spär kəl) to give off sparks or flashes of light [The waves sparkle in the sunlight.] —**sparkles, sparkled, sparkling**

spell (spel) to say the letters in a word [Les could spell many words.] —**spells, spelled, spelling**

splash (splash) to make a liquid scatter and fall in drops [Don't splash water on the floor.] —**splashes, splashed, splashing**

spoil (spoil) **1** to ruin [If you tell anyone, you'll spoil the surprise.] **2** to rot [The fruit will spoil in a few days.] **3** to cause someone to want too much from others [I wish Grandma would not spoil you.] —**spoils, spoiled, spoiling**

spread (spred) to open out or stretch out, in space or time [The duck spread its wings.] —**spreads, spread, spreading**

sprout (sprout) to begin to grow [The seed will sprout in a few days.] —**sprouts, sprouted, sprouting**

stamp (stamp) to bring one's foot down with force [Please don't stamp in the puddle.] —**stamps, stamped, stamping**

a	**a**sk, f**a**t
ā	**a**pe, d**a**te
ä	c**a**r, l**o**t
e	**e**lf, t**e**n
ē	**e**ven, m**ee**t
i	**i**s, h**i**t
ī	**i**ce, f**i**re
ō	**o**pen, g**o**
ô	l**aw**, h**o**rn
oi	**oi**l, p**oi**nt
o͝o	l**oo**k, p**u**ll
o͞o	**oo**ze, t**oo**l
ou	**ou**t, cr**ow**d
u	**u**p, c**u**t
ʉ	f**u**r, f**e**rn
ə	**a** in ago **e** in agent **e** in father **i** in unity **o** in collect **u** in focus
ch	**ch**in, ar**ch**
ŋ	ri**ng**, si**ng**er
sh	**sh**e, da**sh**
th	**th**in, tru**th**
th	**th**en, fa**th**er
zh	**s** in plea**s**ure

stand (stand) to be or get into an upright position on one's feet [Stand by your desk.] —**stands, stood, standing**

start (stärt) to begin to go, do, act, or be [The show will start at 8:30.] —**starts, started, starting**

stick (stik) **1** a small branch or twig [We picked up every stick in the yard.] —**sticks** **2** to press a sharp point into something [Stick this toothpick into the sandwich.] **3** to fasten, as with glue [The stamp will not stick to my letter.] **4** to stay close [Stick with me at the zoo.] —**sticks, stuck, sticking**

still (stil) **1** quiet [The woods were very still.] **2** until now [Are you still playing the same game?]

stop (stäp) to keep from going on, moving, or acting [Stop the car.] —**stops, stopped, stopping**

story[1] (stôr ē) a telling of something; a tale [We all loved the story about the dancing bear.] —**stories**

story[2] (stôr ē) a floor in a building [The elevator stops at the ninth story.] —**stories**

straw (strô) **1** hollow stalks of wheat, rye, or other cereal plants [The hat was woven out of straw.] **2** a slender tube of paper or plastic, used for drinking [She drank her milk through a straw.] —**straws**

stray (strā) to wander from a certain place [Cats may stray from home.] —**strays, strayed, straying**

stream (strēm) a body of flowing water [We crossed the stream on stepping stones.] —**streams**

a	**a**sk, f**a**t
ā	**a**pe, d**a**te
ä	c**a**r, l**o**t
e	**e**lf, t**e**n
ē	**e**ven, m**ee**t
i	**i**s, h**i**t
ī	**i**ce, f**i**re
ō	**o**pen, g**o**
ô	l**aw**, h**o**rn
ơi	**oi**l, p**oi**nt
ơo	l**oo**k, p**u**ll
ōō	**oo**ze, t**oo**l
ou	**ou**t, cr**ow**d
u	**u**p, c**u**t
ʉ	f**u**r, f**e**rn
ə	**a** in ago **e** in agent **e** in father **i** in unity **o** in collect **u** in focus
ch	**ch**in, ar**ch**
ŋ	ri**ng**, si**ng**er
sh	**sh**e, da**sh**
th	**th**in, tru**th**
th	**th**en, fa**th**er
zh	**s** in plea**s**ure

strike (strīk) **1** to hit [Strike the ball when it comes to you.] **2** to stop working to get something [The workers will strike on Monday.] —**strikes, struck, striking**

stuck (stuk) pressed a sharp point into [He stuck his finger with a needle.]

such (such) so much [I had such fun at school!]

sweep (swēp) to clean, usually by brushing with a broom [Please sweep the floor.] —**sweeps, swept, sweeping**

swim (swim) to move in the water by moving arms, legs, fins, or tail [Dan is learning to swim in the pool.] —**swims, swam, swum, swimming**

table (tā bəl) a piece of furniture with a flat top and legs [We ate at the kitchen table.] —**tables**

tack (tak) **1** a short nail with a flat head and sharp point [This tack fell off the bulletin board.] —**tacks 2** to fasten with tacks [Tack this sign to the post.] —**tacks, tacked, tacking**

talk (tôk) **1** to say words [That parrot can really talk!] —**talks, talked, talking 2** the act of saying words [We need to have a talk.] —**talks**

tall (tôl) not low or short [That tower is so tall that I cannot see the top of it.] —**taller, tallest**

tame (tām) no longer wild [The man kept a tame wolf.] —**tamer, tamest**

tape (tāp) **1** a sticky, narrow piece of cloth or plastic [Use this tape to wrap the gift.] **2** a narrow strip of plastic used to record sounds [Let's play the tape that has our favorite songs.] —**tapes 3** to wrap with tape [We will tape the box shut.] **4** to record on tape [Did you tape Steve's song?] —**tapes, taped, taping**

tent

teach (tēch) to show or help to learn how to do something [Will you teach me to skate?] —**teaches, taught, teaching**

team (tēm) a group of people playing together against another group [Tina is on the swim team.] —**teams**

tell (tel) **1** to say [Tell me your name.] **2** to give the story [That book will tell you about the Pilgrims' first Thanksgiving.] —**tells, told, telling**

tent (tent) a canvas shelter [Linda's tent had room for six campers.] —**tents**

then (*th*en) the time after; next [The show ended, and then we went home.]

they (*th*ā) the people or animals being talked about [Joel's parents did not say when they would be home.]

they're (*th*er) they are [They're going to be surprised.]

thick (thik) great in width or depth from side to side [A thick wall surrounded the garden.] —**thicker, thickest**

thin (thin) not wide or deep; not thick [Norm did not skate on the thin ice.] —**thinner, thinnest**

think (thiŋk) to use the mind [We must think of a plan.] —**thinks, thought, thinking**

those (*th*ōz) people or things mentioned [Are those your books?]

threw (thro͞o) sent through the air by a fast motion of the arm [Mike threw the ball to Ed.]

tie (tī) **1** to bind with string, rope, or cord [You may tie the tire swing to this tree.] **2** a piece of cloth men wear around their neck [John's tie is red with black dots.] **3** when the scores of two teams are the same [Beth hopes her team will be able to break the tie.] —**ties, tied, tying**

tiny (tī nē) very small [A tiny ant ran under the leaf.] —**tinier, tiniest**

tired (tīrd) worn out [Lee was tired after the game.]

to (to͞o) **1** in the direction of [Lean to the left.] **2** onto [Paste the stamp to the envelope.]

toast (tōst) bread that has been heated and browned [I like eggs and toast for breakfast.] —**toast**

today (tə dā) on this day [Today is my birthday.]

toe (tō) one of the five parts at the end of a foot [I have a blister on my toe.] —**toes**

together (to͞o ge*th* ər) with one another [Let's walk to the store together.]

too (to͞o) **1** also [Todd laughed and Fran did, too.] **2** more than enough [These boxes are too heavy to carry.]

took (to͝ok) **1** got by force [The bigger girl took the toy away.] **2** called for; needed [This recipe took all the flour we had.] **3** carried [Jake took his book with him.]

tooth (to͞oth) any of the bony, white parts in the mouth used for biting and chewing [Toya lost her tooth in school.] —**teeth**

tower (tou ər) a building that is much higher than it is wide or long [The castle had a tower.] —**towers**

a	**a**sk, f**a**t
ā	**a**pe, d**a**te
ä	c**a**r, l**o**t
e	**e**lf, t**e**n
ē	**e**ven, m**ee**t
i	**i**s, h**i**t
ī	**i**ce, f**i**re
ō	**o**pen, g**o**
ô	l**aw**, h**o**rn
oi	**oi**l, p**oi**nt
o͝o	l**oo**k, p**u**ll
o͞o	**oo**ze, t**oo**l
ou	**ou**t, cr**ow**d
u	**u**p, c**u**t
ʉ	f**u**r, f**e**rn
ə	**a** in ago **e** in agent **e** in father **i** in unity **o** in collect **u** in focus
ch	**ch**in, ar**ch**
ŋ	ri**ng**, si**ng**er
sh	**sh**e, da**sh**
th	**th**in, tru**th**
th	**th**en, fa**th**er
zh	**s** in plea**s**ure

toy (toi) a plaything [That rattle is the baby's favorite toy.] —**toys**

trade (trād) to give one thing for another [Neil will trade baseball cards with you.] —**trades, traded, trading**

trail (trāl) a path formed when people or animals pass [We formed a trail up the mountain.] —**trails**

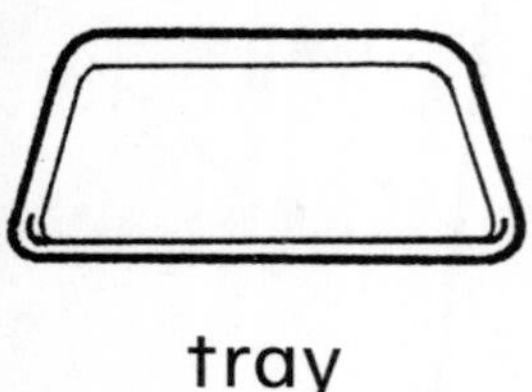

tray

tray (trā) a flat item used for carrying food or other things [The dentist keeps his tools on a metal tray.] —**trays**

trim (trim) **1** to cut or clip [Keesha will trim the dead branches off the tree.] **2** to decorate [Will you help us trim the Christmas tree?] —**trims, trimmed, trimming**

trip (trip) **1** to stumble or cause to stumble [Do not trip over the log.] **2** a journey, especially a short one [We took a trip to the zoo.] —**trips, tripped, tripping**

truck (truk) a large vehicle used to carry loads [Pedro will load the truck.] —**trucks**

true (tro͞o) **1** correct; not false [We know that her story was true.] **2** loyal [James is a true friend.] —**truer, truest**

trunk (trunk) **1** the main stem of a tree [An oak tree has a long, straight trunk.] **2** an elephant's snout [The elephant picked up the peanut with his trunk.] **3** a large box for storing things [I found this old hat in the trunk.] **4** the space in the rear of the car [I locked the groceries in the trunk.] —**trunks**

tube (to͞ob) a long, slender container [She bought a tube of toothpaste.] —**tubes**

a	**a**sk, f**a**t
ā	**a**pe, d**a**te
ä	c**a**r, l**o**t
e	**e**lf, t**e**n
ē	**e**ven, m**ee**t
i	**i**s, h**i**t
ī	**i**ce, f**i**re
ō	**o**pen, g**o**
ô	l**aw**, h**o**rn
oi	**oi**l, p**oi**nt
o͝o	l**oo**k, p**u**ll
o͞o	**oo**ze, t**oo**l
ou	**ou**t, cr**ow**d
u	**u**p, c**u**t
ʉ	f**u**r, f**e**rn
ə	**a** in ago **e** in agent **e** in father **i** in unity **o** in collect **u** in focus
ch	**ch**in, ar**ch**
ŋ	ri**ng**, si**ng**er
sh	**sh**e, da**sh**
th	**th**in, tru**th**
th	**th**en, fa**th**er
zh	**s** in plea**s**ure

tug (tug) **1** pull with force [Watch that the baby does not tug the tablecloth.] **2** to tow with a tugboat [Did you see them tug the barge?] **—tugs, tugged, tugging**

tumble (tum bəl) to do somersaults, handsprings, or other tricks of an acrobat [The children tumble on the mat.] **—tumbles, tumbled, tumbling**

tune (to͞on) a song [The old man hummed my favorite tune.] **—tunes**

turn (turn) **1** to move something around [Turn the key toward the left.] **2** to change [The rain may turn to snow.] **—turns, turned, turning** **3** chance to do something [Everyone will have a turn to ride the horse.] **—turns**

turtle (turt l) a slow-moving animal that has a hard outer shell [Mark keeps the turtle in the box.] **—turtles**

two (to͞o) the number after one [There are two shoes in a pair.]

uncle (uŋ kəl) the brother of one's father or mother [My uncle is Mom's big brother.] **—uncles**

unhappy (un hap ē) sad [Pam is unhappy about the weather.] **—unhappier, unhappiest**

unhook (un ho͝ok) to unfasten a hook [He had to unhook the gate to enter the yard.] **—unhooks, unhooked, unhooking**

unkind (un kīnd) hurting someone's feelings [Rosa has never said an unkind word to anyone.]

unlike (un līk) different [This new car is unlike our old one.]

unlock (un läk) to open with a key [Please unlock the door.] **—unlocks, unlocked, unlocking**

unsafe (un sāf) dangerous [That broken ladder is unsafe to climb.]

untie (un tī) to take apart a knot or bow [He likes to untie his shoes.] —**unties, untied, untying**

use (yo͞oz) **1** to put into action [You may use my radio.] **2** do away with [Try not to use up all of the toothpaste.] —**uses, used, using**

walk (wôk) **1** to move along on foot [Walk on the sidewalk.] **2** the act of walking [Norman went for a long walk.] —**walks, walked, walking**

wall (wôl) the flat side of a room or a building [Linda hung her painting on a wall.] —**walls**

want (wänt) to wish or long for [I want dessert.] —**wants, wanted, wanting**

warm (wôrm) **1** feeling a little heat [This blanket keeps me warm.] **2** showing strong feeling [Her smile was warm and friendly.] —**warmer, warmest**

whale

waterfall (wôt ər fôl) a steep fall of water [Niagara Falls is a large waterfall on the Niagara River.] —**waterfalls**

week (wēk) seven days [It will take a week to do this job.] —**weeks**

were (wʉr) had been [The birds were singing.]

we're (wir *or* wē ər) we are [Here's the tree house that we're building.]

weren't (wʉrnt) were not [They weren't home when we arrived.]

we've (wēv) we have [We've been roller skating all morning.]

whale (hwāl) a very large sea mammal [The whale swam close to our boat.] —**whales**

what (hwut) **1** which thing [What is your name?] **2** so much [What a big mess this is!]

wheat (hwēt) the cereal grass whose grain is used in making the most common type of flour [The fields of wheat stretched for miles.]

when (hwen) at what time [When did you eat breakfast?]

where (hwer) at what place [Where are my glasses?]

whip (hwip) **1** a rod with a strip of leather at one end [The lion tamer carried a whip.] —**whips** **2** to beat into a froth [I helped Mom whip the cream for the dessert.] —**whips, whipped, whipping**

who (ho͞o) what person or persons [Who made this big mess?]

whole (hōl) in one piece; entire [Wanda ate a whole box of cereal.]

why (hwī) for what reason [Why did he go home?]

wide (wīd) long from side to side [The box was too wide to fit through the door.] —**wider, widest**

will (wil) a word that shows that something is yet to be done [Darla will call you soon.]

win (win) to get by work or skill [Tom wants to win the award.] —**wins, won, winning**

wind[1] (wīnd) to turn or coil something around itself [George will wind the kite string.] —**winds, wound, winding**

wind[2] (wind) air that is moving [The wind blew my hat away.] —**winds**

wire (wīr) metal that has been pulled into a very long, thin thread [A fence of barbed wire kept the cattle in.] —**wires**

wish (wish) to want [I wish I could see you soon.] —**wishes, wished, wishing**

a	**a**sk, f**a**t
ā	**a**pe, d**a**te
ä	c**a**r, l**o**t
e	**e**lf, t**e**n
ē	**e**ven, m**ee**t
i	**i**s, h**i**t
ī	**i**ce, f**i**re
ō	**o**pen, g**o**
ô	l**aw**, h**o**rn
oi	**oi**l, p**oi**nt
o͝o	l**oo**k, p**u**ll
o͞o	**oo**ze, t**oo**l
ou	**ou**t, cr**ow**d
u	**u**p, c**u**t
ʉ	f**u**r, f**e**rn
ə	**a** in ago **e** in agent **e** in father **i** in unity **o** in collect **u** in focus
ch	**ch**in, ar**ch**
ŋ	ri**ng**, si**ng**er
sh	**sh**e, da**sh**
th	**th**in, tru**th**
th	**th**en, fa**th**er
zh	**s** in plea**s**ure

won (wun) gotten by work or skill [Do you know who won first prize?]

wood (wood) **1** the hard material of a tree [We need wood for the fire.] **2** lumber [We used wood and nails to build the fort.] —**woods**

wool (wool) yarn, cloth, or clothing made from the hair of sheep, goats, or llamas [That sweater is made of very soft wool.]

word (wurd) a group of letters that mean something [Can you read that word?] —**words**

work (wurk) **1** using energy or skill to make or do something [Farming is hard work.] **2** one's job [Mom left for work.] **3** to do what something is supposed to do [This old radio does not work.] —**works, worked, working**

world (wurld) the Earth [Sonja wants to travel around the world.] —**worlds**

worm (wurm) a small, creeping animal with a soft, slender body, no legs, and no backbone [There is a worm under the leaf.] —**worms**

worth (wurth) the value of something [That vase is worth a lot of money.]

write (rīt) to form letters or words with a pencil or a pen [Rick will write his name down on paper for you.] —**writes, wrote, written, writing**

yet (yet) up to now [He is not gone yet.]

you (yōō) the person or people talked to [You are my best friend.]

you'll (yōōl) you will or you shall [You'll be the first to know.]

you've (yōōv) you have [You've got to do your homework.]